"Run . . . DON'T walk to get this book if you want to grow your staging company! I met Liz several years ago at a RESA conference. I immediately fell in love! Within the first few minutes, I knew she was one of the top staging industry professionals. Her knowledge of the industry and building a successful business has been pivotal in helping me grow my own business. Her RESA classes gave me with an astounding amount of knowledge that I could immediately apply to my business. I recommend this book to anyone who wants the blueprint to make a staging company a success."

—**Tiffany Hardgrave**, Masterpiece Staging & Design

"We own a successful staging business in Florida and have attended several of Liz's professional webinars. This book is a must read for any stager who wants to grow and sell their home staging business. Liz's formula for building and selling a million-dollar staging business is spot-on."

—**Anne and Patrick Furlow**, Step by Stage Interiors

"I've had the pleasure of knowing Liz for twelve+ years and have hired her and her staging company many times. Liz is a gifted leader who is incredibly knowledgeable and talented. When it comes to business, she is smart, savvy, creative, and relatable. When you encounter her presentations and teaching, you will experience the best in the business."

—**Becky Jecha**, Real Estate Professional

"I've known Liz for over fifteen years and have partnered with her on numerous presentations to home sellers and real estate professionals. Her company staged all my real estate listings, and they sold quickly and for top dollar."

—**Lauren Johnson**, Lux Life Real Estate

YOU DON'T KNOW
WHAT
YOU DON'T KNOW™

YOU DON'T KNOW WHAT YOU DON'T KNOW™

BUILDING A MILLION-DOLLAR HOME STAGING BUSINESS AND SELLING IT FOR TOP DOLLAR

ELIZABETH CONNOLLY
STEVEN DENNY

Stonebrook Publishing
Saint Louis, Missouri

A STONEBROOK PUBLISHING BOOK

Copyright ©2021 Elizabeth Connolly and Steven Denny

All rights reserved. Published in the United States by Stonebrook Publishing, a division of Stonebrook Enterprises, LLC, Saint Louis, Missouri. No part of this book may be reproduced, scanned, or distributed in any printed or electronic form without written permission from the author.

Please do not participate in or encourage piracy of copyrighted materials in violation of the author's rights.

Library of Congress Control Number: 2021910011

Paperback ISBN: 978-1-7370312-9-1
Hardback ISBN: 978-1-955711-00-5

www.stonebrookpublishing.net
PRINTED IN THE UNITED STATES OF AMERICA

CONTENTS

Preface 1

Introduction 3

PART 1: Build the Staging Business of Your Dreams 7

    CHAPTER 1: In the Beginning 9

    CHAPTER 2: Creating Your Business Plan 23

    CHAPTER 3: Developing Systems and Procedures 29

    CHAPTER 4: Getting the Right People on Your Bus 37

    CHAPTER 5: Working on the Business 45

PART 2: Stage to Sell for the Highest Possible Amount 49

    CHAPTER 6: Advanced Planning 51

    CHAPTER 7: Deciding to Sell 55

    CHAPTER 8: The Path to Selling Your Staging Business 63

    CHAPTER 9: The Informational Documents 81

    CHAPTER 10: Choose Your Successor 89

CHAPTER 11: Getting the Deal Done **103**

CHAPTER 12: FINALE! Enjoying the Rewards **123**

Acknowledgments **125**

About the Authors **129**

About You Don't Know What You Don't Know™ **133**

PREFACE

The home staging industry is still considered a fairly new industry. The industry has been around for over twenty years but only began to be noticed in 2005. There are currently thousands of home staging companies around the world.

There are two types of home stagers. The first is the individual specializing in preparing an owner-occupied home for sale. This person assesses the property and provides the seller with recommendations and instructions relating to getting the home market-ready. Generally, the seller's furnishings are utilized in this process, with the home staging professional providing advice and often accessories and artwork to enhance and improve upon the items currently in the home.

The second, and the one this book is best geared toward, is the vacant home staging professional. In this profession, the home stager provides the homeowner with recommendations of cosmetic items that need to be undertaken prior to the sale of the vacant home. Additionally, she provides furnishings, area rugs, artwork, lamps, plants, and accessories to accentuate the architecture of the home and appeal to the buyer demographic that will be considering purchasing the property. A significant amount of planning and preparation is involved in opening a vacant home staging business. I would be remiss if I didn't mention that many successful home staging companies offer both occupied as well as vacant home staging services, design services, residential renovation services, and much more. No matter which type of business you have, this book will be of significant benefit in guiding you in the sale of your company.

INTRODUCTION

YOU MAY BE TEMPTED TO SKIP THIS INTRO. I'm an avid reader, and when I have a new book, I want to get right to the essence of the story. Many times, I have skipped the introduction only to have to go back after a chapter or two to garner the foundation of the story. That's what this intro is: the foundation you need, the backstory, to building and selling a successful staging business. **DON'T SKIP THIS INTRO.**

Good for you! You have decided to sell your home staging business. The thing most people don't consider is the fact that, to sell a business, you need to go back to the very beginning, the point when starting your home staging business was only a dream. Doesn't make sense, right? You have been running your business for years, and now, you are moving on to another phase of your life plan. You want to sell your business for the highest amount possible, and you want to do it *now*. This book is your roadmap to a successful sale and an insider's guide to getting more than you ever thought possible when selling your business.

The most successful business sales are those businesses that have a strong track record of planning, processes and procedures, record keeping, and most importantly, accurate financial and accounting records. Before you put your business up for sale and announce it to the public, there are steps you need to take to assure that you are selling to the right person, at the right price, with the right terms that benefit both you and the buyer, and most importantly that you have a strategic tax plan in place prior to signing the sales contract—in essence, an exit strategy.

In the general scheme of things, home staging is a fairly new industry. Many accountants and business brokers have never dealt with a home staging business, and therefore, have a very limited understanding of what we do. I was fortunate we had been working with the same accounting firm since the inception of our business in 2007, and the firm worked with us to prepare a "business dashboard." The business dashboard is very similar to a business plan. During quarterly meetings with the accounting firm, our dashboard was analyzed, tweaked, and adjusted based on current market trends. Over a twelve-year period, our accounting firm aided us in sales projections, cash flow, and, most importantly, the tax ramifications of small business ownership.

In 2018, my husband retired, and the family began talking about selling the business and moving to Florida. We asked our accountant to prepare a business valuation to see where we stood. We spent around $3,000 for said valuation and were extremely surprised that the valuation of our profitable home staging business came in much lower than expected. We quickly learned that many more factors are taken into consideration in the sale of a business than just the fact that you have had sustained growth over a twelve-year period with well over $1 million in annual revenue.

Shortly after we received this valuation, I was at a networking event and heard the term, *business broker*. A business broker is the liaison who not only provides a

Introduction

true valuation of your business but also creates the marketing package for the sale and confidentially secures, interviews, and vets potential buyers. There is a plethora of front-end work on your end (the seller) that needs to be provided to the business broker before your company can be marketed to potential buyers. The stronger your records (and track record), the easier it will be to compile all of the data needed to put together a comprehensive, appealing marketing package and thereby secure you the highest possible sale price for your company.

My business broker, Steven Denny, acknowledged that we had the most comprehensive systems, procedures, and records that he had ever seen during his many years of brokering the sale of various businesses. Those systems and records were of significant importance in assessing the value of our company. While the accountant had the "numbers" to create the valuation, he did not have the all-encompassing knowledge of the various components that are taken into consideration when assigning a value to a business.

Many would consider the business broker an unnecessary step and a significant expense. I will tell you personally that my business sold for more than twice the valuation provided by the accountant who knew my business numbers inside and out.

As with any business transaction, it is important to have documents prepared and reviewed by a competent attorney. Did you know there are attorneys who specialize solely in the sale of small businesses? A savvy accountant is another component in the sale of your business. We were amazed to learn the difference between an "asset sale" and "personal goodwill." The difference in the tax percentages in these two categories is huge.

There is so much you need to know to navigate the sale of your business. Just as in running a successful staging business, it takes a team. Be sure you have the right team in place before attempting to sell. This book takes you through the steps required to build *and sell* your business. I realize that if you have picked up this book, you have most likely already built your business. With that in mind, once you have read through the steps it takes for a solid foundation, you might want to put off the sale until you have "beefed up" some areas of weakness. Taking this step will help you increase the value of your business. Time is money. If you move too quickly, you can leave money on the table. **Now, let's start at the beginning.**

PART 1

Build the Staging Business of Your Dreams

IN THE BEGINNING

*"Every accomplishment starts
with the decision to try."*
—John F. Kennedy

As my twelfth year of owning a successful home staging business came to a close, I began reflecting on how the industry had changed and grown. When I started INhance IT! back in 2007, I had no idea how the industry would explode. Nor did I envision building a company that would not only provide a wonderful career for my daughter but also one for my son-in-law and five fabulous employees.

Looking back on our humble beginnings, I am in awe of what we built. My daughter and I started the company with $5,000 (provided by my husband) and a prayer. At the time, we were a bit oblivious—we didn't know what we didn't know—but we had a strong foundation of ready, willing, and able home-building clients from day one.

A funny story comes to mind regarding our first two vacant staging projects. I was in a meeting at the local

Home Builder's Association, and as we were going around the room sharing the latest industry news, I shared that I had left the home builder who I had been working for and had started a home staging company. One of the builders immediately said, "That's great! I have two spec homes ready to go. How soon can you get them staged?" Holy smokes! We were off and running, and we hadn't yet purchased one piece of furniture. We scheduled installation for the following week and went directly to a local furniture store after the meeting. We discovered pretty quickly that $5,000 doesn't go far and that we had to be creative.

In the early days, we were working out of my basement. We were set up with two desks and computers and a file cabinet. We had no warehouse, dock, or receiving area for inventory. Based on that, we scheduled the furniture to be delivered directly to the two spec homes. Fortunately for us, they were right next door to one another. Two delivery guys began bringing in boxes. Uh oh! The stuff wasn't assembled. We sweet-talked them into helping us assemble the stuff (with the offer of a really big tip), which got them behind schedule. Luckily, they were independent contractors for the furniture store, and it was their own truck. We befriended these guys (Randy and Billy) and arranged for them to be our regular contract movers. The builder was impressed with what we accomplished and immediately booked us to stage three additional properties. I would be embarrassed to present that staging today. But, as with any industry, there was a learning curve, and we continued to evolve and build our brand.

There were two factors that came into play for us back in 2007. The first was that there were only two other

In the Beginning

companies in our area offering vacant home staging, and quite frankly, their furnishings and design plans were very dated. That gave us a leg up. In fact, that is the main reason we started INhance IT! We knew that we could provide a fresh, new, transitional look that had never been offered in the Saint Louis market.

The second factor was that the economy was tanking. Yes, tanking! You may ask, "Why start a business in a bad economy?" A bad economy is good for the staging industry, and this was especially true back in 2007 through 2010. During that time, homes were sitting on the market for months on end.

In the early years, our key client base consisted of home builders. Prior to 2006, the home building industry enjoyed a very robust run. Builders couldn't build homes fast enough, and land was at a premium. Many top builders began increasing their levels of inventory (speculative) homes that were available for immediate move-in. The year 2006 was pivotal for the Saint Louis home-building industry. During fourth quarter 2005 through second quarter 2006, a plethora of inventory homes began flooding the market. During the years leading up to this, financing a home was easy, and just about anyone could get a loan. As lending industry regulations became more stringent, fewer people were able to secure loans, and speculative homes began sitting on the market for months.

At one point in 2006, the builder I worked for had sixty-three inventory properties. That's a lot of cash tied up. As director of sales and marketing, it fell upon me to come up with creative ways to move these homes. We brainstormed as a team and focused on the fact that many of the visitors to our display (showcase) homes stated, "We're only here to look at the decorating." We figured that if they like decorating so much, why not decorate the spec homes? Hopefully, that would get potential buyers through the doors. The problem was, we didn't own any extra furniture.

This is when I first learned of the term *home staging*. I reached out to one of the two local home staging resources and contracted them to stage several properties. The quality was mediocre, but it was better than an empty house. This was when I began thinking that offering superior home staging services could be a very lucrative business. The stars aligned in December 2006 as I turned the big 5-0 and my daughter graduated from college. It was the perfect time to undertake a new endeavor.

Back in the 2000s, home builders were accustomed to paying thousands of dollars to merchandise (decorate) display homes. The average display home furnishings investment was around $20/sf or $60,000 for a 3,000 square foot home. Many of the higher-end builders budgeted $25+ per square foot. The bottom line is that builders were used to spending money. Now, their cash was tied up in the spec properties.

Coming from a home building background, I saw firsthand how this impacted builders. Many well-known builders were struggling to stay afloat, and by 2008, many began going under. The builders who survived realized they had to look for new solutions. My company, INhance IT! Home Staging, provided these solutions. I put together a program offering to provide long-term rental furnishings for display homes as well as short-term furniture

In the Beginning

rental for spec properties. This allowed builders to spread out their cash flow over a longer period rather than spending over $60,000 in a lump sum to furnish a display.

In the long run, builders ended up paying as much or more for the furniture through their rental fees. However, they didn't have to worry about moving, storage, repair, maintenance, or inventory control. It was a win-win for everyone. Since builders were used to paying exorbitant amounts for furnishings and there was little to no competition, we were able to charge substantial staging fees.

Our initial staging agreements were for nine months. (Remember, the market was in very bad shape as many potential buyers lost thousands, if not millions, of dollars in the stock market downturn.) In today's 2021 market, most staging agreements are for one or two months. Our main competitor (the company that I had previously used for staging) was offering unlimited staging with no money upfront. The furnishings would stay in the house until it sold, whether it was a week or a year or even more, and the staging fee was paid out of escrow at closing.

As a new company, that system would not work for us. We needed cash flow and needed it *now*. We offered nine-month agreements with half payable up front and the balance at closing. Luckily, our fresh new look enticed clients to pay the half up front, but it was certainly a sales job to get them to do so. We quickly began taking credit card payments for the initial installments, which helped us expedite the cash flow process.

As with many industries, home staging evolved and became a household name. Top real estate agents recognized that their staged listings began selling faster and for top dollar, and they began embracing home staging services. Today, it is almost unheard of to allow any portion of the payment out of escrow at closing. Savvy stagers are getting 100% of the staging fee upfront. Back in the day, those of us offering the split payment plan were, in a sense, acting as a banker for the builder or seller. But everyone starts somewhere, right?

Back to that initial $5,000 investment. As I said, it didn't go far! My daughter, Courtney, decided to go all in and put her $25,000 wedding fund into the business. That got us another few houses of inventory. During that time, we couldn't buy furniture fast enough, and we weren't ready to jump into the wholesale purchasing arena. Within the first two months, I took out a $100,000 line of credit. The phone was literally ringing off the hook. There was a new stager in town, and it was INhance IT!

We blew the competition away with our transitional look. We vowed never to put anything in one of our staged properties that wasn't high enough quality for our own personal homes. In fact, in the early days, we were constantly borrowing furniture and accessories from our homes. We would make runs to Home Goods and purchase ten shopping carts full of accessories at a time. The biggest problem was fitting everything into the car. There were many trips where I ended up with bags, footstools, and lampshades piled on my lap. There were times we had so many faux trees in the car that we could barely see out the windows. Courtney had an Envoy, and I had a Cadillac CTS. We quickly traded in our vehicles for two Escalades. We were the luxury stager and wanted to present a luxury

In the Beginning

image. Plus, we could load those ten carts of accessories in our Escalades, no problem.

The next big step was to come up with storage solutions for the furnishings. It wasn't feasible to continue to have furniture delivered directly from the furniture store to the home we were staging. We had about a month of deliveries to the two-car garage of my home, but that did not go over well with my husband. It was March in Missouri, and we had snow—the cars needed to be in the garage.

We were lucky to acquire a 10x20 storage unit at a facility less than a mile from my house. We would have the furniture delivered to my house and then have our moving guys pick it up, assemble items in my garage, and transport it to the storage unit if it wasn't immediately needed for staging. We also needed the storage for times when a house sold, and we didn't have another home ready for move-in. Luckily, that did not happen very often. Nevertheless, we soon needed a second storage unit.

Working out of storage units is an absolute nightmare. No matter how hard you try to stay organized, items get stacked on top of each other and shoved in to make more room for additional furniture, and worst of all, when you need to pull something for a job, you have to move a bunch of stuff to get to the pieces you need. There were a few times when I was buried under fallen mattresses and one time under a hutch that had fallen forward. I even dropped a headboard and broke a bone in my foot. It was time for a better solution.

COURTNEY'S STORY

"Starting a business with my mother was the second-best business decision I have ever made. The best decision was selling that business and moving to paradise!"

Let's start at the beginning. It was my senior year of college. I was studying to obtain a degree in marketing and had no clue what I would do with my life after graduation. One of my big senior projects was to create a fictitious business and put together a business and marketing plan. This project couldn't have been assigned at a more perfect time because Liz had recently approached me about starting a staging business. Of course, I agreed. It sounded fun and easy (ha-ha). Why create a fictitious business when I could create a real plan for my future?

If you know Liz and me, you know that we like to get things done quickly and make decisions fast. We sat down one morning and brainstormed business names, researched local companies, and investigated staging websites. By the end of that day, we bought a domain, had a logo and vision drawn up, and started the business plan. Things took off quickly, and I couldn't wait to graduate and jump into the business full time.

I instantly fell in love with staging and owning a business. The real estate industry is exhilarating, stressful, and tumultuous. Each day brings new challenges to face and new obstacles to work through. When we started, we were learning as we went along by making blunders and navigating the twists and turns that come with a fast-paced, energetic business. We had no formal staging training,

In the Beginning

so we created our own practices and policies as unique situations arose daily.

We did so much research at the beginning but never realized that there was actual training for staging. How did we miss this? When I found out about staging training, I quickly took my first course, and our business took off to a whole new level. Liz followed suit, and soon after, she was writing her own courses and providing training to other stagers. I became dedicated to expanding my knowledge of the staging industry and committed to taking one staging training per year. The more training and classes I took, the more our business grew. Taking staging training was a pivotal step in our business journey.

People always ask, "How is it working with your mom?" and my answer has always been the same: It's priceless!

I think our partnership worked so well because Liz was the leader whom I had the pleasure of learning from. She is the most remarkable woman I have ever met, and no, I'm not just saying that because she is my mother. Anyone that has met her or worked with her would agree that she is a special person. She has the biggest heart and always wants everyone around her to be happy. She would give you the shirt off her back at any time. She has furnished houses and schools for the less fortunate and is constantly giving back to her community, never expecting recognition or anything in return. She wants the best for everyone, and her energy is contagious. Her genuine charismatic personality and happy spirit make her successful at everything she does. She was highly respected in the Saint Louis real estate industry. She was dedicated to the betterment of the industry and volunteered her time and support continuously. Our company was a success because of her.

We did have our rough patches at the beginning, and the first two years were the hardest. I was a pessimistic, naïve, know-it-all new college grad, and Liz was a positive professional leader, so we butted heads quite a bit. We had days where we would disagree on almost everything and days where we needed a break from each other. We had disagreements on where a sofa should be placed or if we needed that extra piece of art in the bedroom, but at the end of the day, these disagreements made us stronger, and we pushed each other to make INhance IT! the best that we possibly could.

Once we learned how to work with each other (and I grew up), it was smooth sailing. We took a DISC assessment, grasped how similar we were, and learned how to navigate our differences in a positive way. Most of the time, we were on the same page with things, even though we still had silly disagreements about a living room setup, using faux fruit, or setting a dining table.

Having your mom as a business partner is incredible. We got to shop together, "play house" (as Liz would say) together, network together, take lunch breaks together, and most of all, build an empire together. I loved spending every day working with my best friend and doing what we loved. I am so grateful that I had the privilege to learn from Liz. She taught me how to run a business and about success, gratitude, marketing, customer service, organization, and life. The things I learned from her during our thirteen years in business are priceless, and I wouldn't trade them for anything. We both thought we would be running INhance IT! for life. INhance IT! was our life, and we loved it, and our spouses supported us and the hours we devoted to the company.

WORKING WITH MY HUSBAND

We put a lot of thought into bringing my husband, Jon, into the family business. Hiring him was a great decision for us and the company. Jon brought his master Excel skills, tech-support abilities, and customer service qualities to the business, and Liz and I got to focus more on the part we loved: the staging.

Luckily, Jon and I are pretty much complete opposites. Jon is easygoing, laid back, calm, and likes to put on a pair of headphones and do his thing. This worked very well for us because he levels out my unique personality. There were some days that work came home with us, and we would spend hours talking about clients or issues, but for the most part, we kept it in the office. I can only recall a handful of times when we had a disagreement, mostly about his lack of use of the Google calendar.

It is an interesting dynamic having the people you love the most around 24/7, but it worked for us, and I loved it.

One of my favorite things about running our own staging company was when our daughter, Olive, came into the office or to a staging install. She would set up shop in the accessory room at the office and pretend to stage. She would make flower arrangements, set tables, and count glassware. At staging installs, she would fluff pillows, unwrap furniture, and place accessories on tables. She loved being part of the team and would always say, "I want to be a stager when I grow up." Spending this precious time with her and letting her experience strong women kicking ass is a lesson she will always treasure.

Some days, we even had the pleasure of having my dad, John, in the office. He was (and still is) the best handyman. He would do a multitude of odd jobs and was happy to be paid with a lunch. In the beginning, we took over his basement, including his pool table, for several years. He never complained and only asked for a small section for his TV and golf equipment. He was also great at lending a hand and would help carry heavy accessories, build shelving, and keep us organized.

Having a family business was a blessing for us. We got to spend quality time together, learn together, and grow together, all while having fun and building our empire. I credit all our success and accomplishment to building our team with family, trust in each other, and trust in God. It's not always easy, but it's always worth it.

SELLING THE FAMILY BUSINESS

Deep breath. I still get emotional thinking about selling the family business. When you start something from the bottom and nurture it for years, it becomes your baby, your life. It's like sending your only child to college; you know you did an incredible job raising her, but it's time to let her shine on her own.

It's bittersweet to think about someone else taking over and making your business their own. It's hard to even imagine. I cried more than I want to admit and questioned our decision a thousand times. I even thought about pulling out and continuing to run the business. But that's not what I wanted. I wanted to live at the beach with my

In the Beginning

family. I was done with the stress, done with the turbulent real estate industry, done with being available 24/7, and done with managing employees. Those things were not making me happy anymore, and I wanted happiness. I wanted freedom! That was my "why" for selling.

After we made that huge decision, what did we do next? We didn't even know where to start. Thankfully, we hired an amazing business broker who took the stress off us and ultimately sold our business for more than we thought was possible. He helped us understand our value and the worth of the business we built together.

Luckily, like I said before, Liz is an incredible businesswoman. She had all the essential documents and operation details prepared. Everything just needed to be put together professionally, priced right, and marketed effectively. It was a lot of work. Think of it as staging your business. You want to put your best foot forward for your potential buyers and have everything cleaned up and ready to go to ensure a smooth transition. You want your buyer to see how much you loved your business but also envision themselves operating as the owner. You want the buyer to see your client base and trust that the relationships you built will be strong enough to persevere through the sale. And you want the buyer to have a clear picture of exactly how you ran things so that they have a jumping-off point and can keep the company running smoothly after the transition.

The entire journey was an emotional roller coaster. It was difficult and sad. It was confusing and meticulous. It was joyous and exhilarating. You are leaving behind your legacy that will now be someone else's. But at the end of the day, it was the right decision. It was freedom.

I am grateful for the experience of not only running a wildly successful staging business but also for being fortunate enough to sell the thriving business and follow my dreams with my best friend and partner by my side. As I continue my work leading the staging industry into the future, I hope all business owners look at their company daily and ask themselves, "Do I love what I am doing? Am I fulfilled?" If not, find a way to make a change. Open your mind to possibilities and open your heart to allow and accept good things into your life.

My advice for after the sale is this: cut the cord. Let go. Do not follow the new business on social media or talk to previous clients about the new owners' changes. Let go and be at peace with your decision. You will not get the closure you want and deserve if you are agonizing over the new owners' decisions and modifications to the business. It's not yours to worry about anymore. This is considerably more difficult than it sounds and will likely take time and consistent discipline, but trust me, let go and move on. Be free!

As you can see, starting a staging business is a work in progress. Depending on the depth of your pockets (cash on hand) and level of experience, you'll most likely experience some growing pains. That's why it is imperative to have a strong business plan before you start a business, which leads us to Chapter 2: Creating Your Business Plan.

CREATING YOUR BUSINESS PLAN

*"Don't borrow someone else's plan.
Develop your own philosophy, and it will
lead you to unique places."*
—Jim Rohn

"If you fail to plan, you are planning to fail."
—Benjamin Franklin

The business plan is your detailed description of the business you expect to build. The value of the business plan is that it provides you with a roadmap to your planned destination. But remember, this is a plan based on the knowledge you have to date. Your business plan will not be perfect but will contain all your thinking and planning, and it will also guide you to additional research you may have to do. No plans are perfect. They are not supposed to be because you don't know what you don't know. You should approach the preparation of your plan as a guide containing everything you can imagine and the provision for change to reflect what actually happens.

The body of the business plan can be divided into four distinct sections:

1. Executive summary
2. Description of the business
3. Marketing plan
4. Financial management plan

Your plan should also include various supporting documents and detailed financial projections.

SECTION 1: EXECUTIVE SUMMARY

This should be the short story you tell your friends and closest advisors about your business. It explains the fundamentals in a summarized format. Imagine you have two minutes to tell someone all about your business. Write it down and make it two pages or less. This is your executive summary, which may be a key part of your application for a loan or other capital.

SECTION 2: DESCRIPTION OF THE BUSINESS

In this section, provide a detailed description of your business. An excellent question to ask yourself is: What business am I in? In answering this question, include your products, market, and services, as well as a thorough description of what makes your business unique. Remember, however, that as you develop your business plan, you may have to modify or revise your initial questions. Here are specifics that should be included:

Business Overview

Offer a description of the business, including:

- The legal structure (LLC, Corporation, etc.)
- Business formation history
- The type of business
- Location
- Means of doing business (internet, mail order, etc.)

Operations Plan

Offer an explanation describing how the business will function, including the physical setup and responsibilities for each specific task.

Products and Services

Describe the services offered. Classify the different types of services and provide a brief description of each.

Management Team

Provide pertinent, concise background information of all key players involved in the business.

SECTION 3: MARKETING PLAN

How well you market the business, along with a few other considerations, will ultimately determine your degree of success or failure. The key element of a successful marketing plan is to know your customers—their likes, dislikes, and expectations. By identifying these factors, you can develop a marketing strategy that will allow you to arouse and fulfill their needs.

Market Analysis

Include an overview of the market as a whole with specific data and charts or graphs. Define your target market and your plans for catering to this specific audience.

Sales and Marketing

Outline pricing and sales information. Include rationalizations for why your audience will buy your services and how you will reach them through marketing and advertising efforts.

Competitive Analysis

Analyze the strengths and weaknesses of your direct and indirect competitors. Demonstrate how you will gain a competitive edge against your competition.

SECTION 4: FINANCIAL MANAGEMENT PLAN

How well you manage the finances of your business is the cornerstone of a successful business venture. A solid financial management plan will not only make your business operation easier but also minimize worry and uncertainty for the leaders and managers. Remember that the foundation of the business value is also determined by its financial performance, so resolve to always manage finances as actively as possible to ensure that you are growing the value of the business over time.

Financial Plan

Include all financial information, from startup costs to balance sheets. The financial section should include:

- The amount necessary to start or maintain the business
- The amount needed over the next two, three, five years
- Planned use of the funds
- Anticipated need for additional funding
- Ongoing business expenses, including salaries, insurance costs, promotional expenses, etc.

Projections

- Provide projected income statements and balance sheets for at least two or three years.
- At the end of your business plan, attach supporting documents, such as articles on the company, resumes of key personnel, awards received, and education/designations.
- Revisit, revisit, revisit! This will be a working document for the life of your business.
- Review all your goals, marketing plans, and financial forecasts on a regular basis.

Succession Plan

- What are your plans for the future?
- Who will take over your business?
- Are you planning to have family members work in the business? Will they want to become owners of the business? You will need to have these discussions early on so you know what direction you will need to take when the time is right.

- Will you have a key employee that may be interested in buying the business?

The US Small Business Administration (SBA.org) has an excellent document with multiple worksheets that you may wish to use as your template. Remember, if you will need a loan or other capital to start up your business, you will need a business plan and a full set of financial projections for your loan application. Many banks and lenders will require you to use the SBA Business Plan as a component of your loan application.

The US Small Business Administration also has a free mentorship group known as SCORE—the Service Corp of Retired Executives. These experienced experts can consult with you on the development of your business plan and point you to additional resources, all free of charge.

DEVELOPING SYSTEMS AND PROCEDURES

*"People of accomplishment rarely sit back
and let things happen to them.
They go out and happen to things."*
—Leonardo da Vinci

As I mentioned in the Introduction, one of the key reasons we were able to sell our business at a higher valuation was because we had very strong systems and procedures. Did we have them when we started in 2007? Not really. At the time we started our staging business, we didn't know that there was staging training available. We relied on our previous business experiences and continually referred to and tweaked our business plan.

SYSTEM 1 – FINANCING YOUR BUSINESS

When you created your business plan, you should have come up with your projected revenues. To achieve these revenues, you basically have to work in reverse.

How much income do you need or want to make this year? Next year? Three to five-year plan? This determines how many houses of furniture you will need to purchase. Initially, you will have to spend money to make money.

Now you know how much money you need, but do you know where you will get this money? Unless you have a large amount of savings or a nice inheritance, you will most likely need a source of financing for your business.

Sources of Financing

- Home equity line of credit. Banks will want some type of collateral on the loan.
- 401K – You can use your own funds tax-free (provided you use a third-party administrator so that the funds used from your retirement savings never move into your personal accounts).
- Loan from family members
- Sell a large-ticket item you no longer need
- SBA Loan – (SCORE consultants can help with this)

As I mentioned in the Introduction, we started our company with $5,000 and a prayer. Our projections showed that there was pent-up demand for our service, but we didn't realize that our initial projections were low. We quickly realized that we had created demand and that we had better be able to serve that demand or we'd lose momentum. Hence, my daughter donating her $25,000

Developing Systems and Procedures

wedding fund and me securing a $100K home equity line of credit. As the saying goes, "Go big or go home."

There are many in the home staging industry who enjoy "decorating homes" and want to dabble in the business. Every individual has their idea of what they expect from their company. If you want to build and sell a million-dollar staging company, you have to be prepared to invest heavily upfront and reinvest profits until you have the assets (inventory) to stage the number of houses needed to reach your target goal.

SYSTEM 2 – ACCOUNTING

It seemed all the stars were aligned at the moment we decided to start our home staging business. The day I went to my bank to open our business accounts, they happened to be having a small business coffee hour. They invited me to stay, and I'm glad I did. The speaker that day was a gentleman from an accounting firm. I was intrigued by his company's unique accounting/business development system called the Business Dashboard. I stayed and chatted with him after the event and set up a time to meet at his office. He asked several questions about aspects of the business I had never considered, and my head was spinning. I immediately signed up with his firm, and the insight and direction that he and his team provided were invaluable.

When you are first starting a business and money is tight, the accounting fees can seem enormous. We signed an agreement that covered monthly meetings, quarterly reports, and annual tax planning and preparation. That way, we knew exactly what we would be spending on these services. It is important to have your CPA in place before you invest in your accounting system. Your accountant will recommend the system that will work best for your business and the system that integrates well with the systems utilized by his office. We opted to go with QuickBooks and then moved to QuickBooks Online.

Whatever accounting system you choose, be sure that you receive comprehensive training before setting up the system. Many times, a person at your accounting firm's office can assist you with this setup. It is important to get off on the right foot or you go back to another adage, "garbage in, garbage out." When you decide to sell your business, you will need several years of financial reports, all of which can be generated through your QuickBooks (or other) accounting system.

Early on in your business, you will want to meet with your CPA on a regular basis. We met monthly the first year to be sure we were on track and that we weren't missing anything. Your CPA will prepare the tax projections for your company and recommend the timing of various asset purchases. If you don't have a strong CPA on your team from the very beginning, you can be setting yourself up for failure. You have most likely started off your business as an LLC. There will come a time when it benefits you tax-wise to file as an S-Corp. If you are married, your joint income and tax return comes into play. Unless you have an accounting degree, you need a tax professional to guide you through these waters. Even if you do have an accounting degree, your CPA keeps up to date on the myriad of new and revised tax laws that come out on a regular basis. **Hire a professional.**

SYSTEM 3 – INVENTORY CONTROL

As mentioned in the Preface, this book is primarily geared toward the home staging businesses focused on vacant staging. Whether you are offering occupied staging, vacant staging, or both, you will need a system to track your inventory. This is imperative for design planning purposes as well as for annual taxation.

When we started our home staging business in 2007, an inventory control system relating to the home staging industry was not readily available. During the initial meeting, our accountant stressed the importance of keeping accurate records of our inventory and purchases. This allowed us to be able to analyze the value of the inventory utilized on each staging job, calculate job costs, and assure profitability.

In this book, the term *inventory* refers to the items utilized to complete a staging project. Inventory includes furnishings, area rugs, artwork, lamps, plants, and accessories. In a traditional business, inventory typically refers to the goods you have on hand for sale. For home stagers, inventory includes the items they own and plan to continue to own to complete multiple staging installations.

As mentioned earlier in the business planning section and financing section, you will need to make inventory projections so you will have inventory on hand to provide the number of projected staging jobs your company will complete during a given time. Each vacant home will require a certain number of sofas, chairs, dining tables, coffee and end tables, beds, nightstands, rugs, artwork, and accessories. Not only will you need to know what you own, but you will need to know where the items are located at any given time. You will also need to know how many "turns" you are getting out of each piece of inventory, which, in turn, will assist in determining your profitability.

In the home staging industry, most accountants consider accessory items an expense of doing business and the furnishings a long-term asset. These are handled in different ways in the course of the accounting process. In many states that require annual personal property tax payments, the long-term assets (furnishings) are taxed on their annual depreciated value.

Your accountant will need to know your asset purchases as well as any sale of assets, donation of assets, or write-offs due to damage and breakage. As your business grows, so does your asset inventory. At one point in our business, we had over 100 vacant homes staged with our assets at any given time. Think about it. A staged home with a living, dining, kitchen, breakfast room, and master bedroom requires an average of 30-plus pieces of furniture. Extrapolate that over 100 homes, and that is a significant amount of assets to track on an ongoing basis.

Luckily, several inventory control systems are now available, relating specifically to the home staging industry. Research all of them and let your accountant determine the one that best fits your business model. It is much easier to start with an inventory system right out of the gate than to go back after the fact and try to capture all your inventory. That is why it is important to get your systems in place before you begin doing business.

Developing Systems and Procedures

Your inventory control system should also be able to track your inventory turns. Turns are the number of times an inventory item is utilized for staging jobs. If you purchase your inventory wisely, you should be able to use it for ten years. The more you use it, the more profit in your pocket. This leads to another factor that will be addressed in the next chapter, Getting the Right People on Your Bus.

CHAPTER 4

GETTING THE RIGHT PEOPLE ON YOUR BUS

"When you're surrounded by people who share a passionate commitment around a common purpose, anything is possible."
—Howard E. Schultz

Another key system in building a successful staging business is your employee manual. A detailed employee manual is imperative once you begin hiring employees. Many stagers start small and don't consider the need for employee systems and end up shooting themselves in the foot and setting themselves up for lawsuits. Even if you are hiring family and friends for your team, it is important that everyone knows their job description and expectations.

YOUR EMPLOYEE MANUAL

Having a comprehensive employee manual was one of the key factors that added to the value of my home staging business. You will need to tweak it as you grow your team, but you definitely need to include the following:

- Mission and vision statement
- Organization chart
- Job descriptions (all positions including your own)
- Dress and hygiene code
- Pay rate
- Timesheets
- Employee benefits
- Employment review policy
- Paid and unpaid holidays
- Vacation/time off policy and forms to request time off
- Moving/warehouse procedure
- Staging processes and procedures
- Checklists

It is a good idea to review the employee manual as part of the interview process. Each of these items should be discussed and help identify any red flags and will assist in determining if the candidate is truly the right person for your bus. It is important to have each employee sign an acknowledgment that they have read and received a copy of the manual. Each time processes and systems are updated or changed, employees should receive a copy of said changes for their manual.

OPERATIONS MANUAL

Having a comprehensive operations manual was a cornerstone in making our business attractive to potential buyers. The operations manual is a comprehensive road map to running your company. It should include everything that is featured in your employee manual along with the following:

- Copy of your EIN document
- Copy of any business licenses
- Copy of your business plan
- Employment ads
- Employment application forms
- Discipline forms
- Timesheets
- Step-by-step details relating to performing each job within the organization
- Training programs
- Details relating to performing all processes and procedures utilized in the organization
- Database of clients
- Database of vendors and suppliers
- Insurance policies

Each time processes and systems are updated or changed, you or your operations manager should be responsible for updating the operations manual.

WHO TO HIRE AND WHEN TO HIRE

Most home stagers start with a limited number of paid employees. With my company, it was just my daughter and myself. Just because it is only you, or you and one other person, doesn't mean you don't need an organization chart. Each of the job duties relating to the business should be included on the chart, even if your name is in every box. Having this outline will allow you to determine which positions need to be filled now and which will come later.

It is a good idea to track your time expenditure. Early in the business, keep a daily log of how much time you are spending in each organization chart category. As your business grows, you will not be able to effectively do everything yourself. You may feel that you can't afford to hire an employee right now but look at the physical and emotional costs involved in doing it alone. Not hiring staff can slow down or prohibit projected business growth. As we stated earlier, it takes a village.

Before you send out your advertisement for employment or post an ad, you will need to hone your interviewing skills. A business owner wears many hats, and some areas of expertise are stronger than others. If you have never been in a position to interview or hire employees, you will need to get educated in this area. A simple internet search can pull up a myriad of information. Read everything you can and conduct some practice interviews with family or friends. The last thing you want to do is come across as unprepared and/or unprofessional when conducting the interview.

The interview sets the tone for your company. As your team grows, other team members like your operations manager or logistics manager may be conducting initial interviews of team members for their areas. Their individual employee manuals should have a section on interviewing and a list of prepared interview questions that are asked of each potential candidate applying for a position. The final decision on adding any team member should come from you, the owner of the company.

Your business plan outlines your company's mission, vision, and values. It is imperative that these are recognized and embraced by any person you add to your team. A candidate may have experience and stellar references but may not be the right fit for your team. If the candidate will be interfacing with multiple team members, it is important that the personalities mesh, or you will be setting everyone up for disappointment and business disruption.

If you are offering vacant staging services, the first team members you need are moving professionals. Over the years, I have seen numerous stagers try to move the furniture themselves, and it simply isn't sustainable in the long term if you want to grow your business. You need a resource for a truck, a driver, and a moving helper. You don't necessarily need to hire these folks in the beginning; you can contract this through a third-party contractor. Just be certain that they are fully insured (both the truck and with workers' compensation). I strongly suggest that you sit down with this third-party resource and review the details of your employee manual relating to job descriptions, dress and hygiene code, moving procedure, checklists, and expectations. They may not be on your payroll, but they are definitely part of your team.

Another factor to take into consideration when determining who to hire is analyzing which areas are your strong suit and looking at what elements of the business you enjoy most. I was strong in networking and sales, and my daughter in employee training and acquiring inventory. We both enjoyed the design and staging installation element most. Neither of us was strong in systems management or accounting. We also found that it was difficult to have phone "sales consultations" while we were on-site installing staging projects.

The first full-time employee we hired was an in-house operations manager. This person handled all of the telephone sales and all of the internal systems relating to the business, including sending out proposals, follow-up, sending contracts, scheduling previews, installations and removals, sending invoices, receiving payments, banking, credit card reconciliation, entering transactions in QuickBooks, inputting new employees into the system, and payroll. This allowed us to do what we enjoyed and, most importantly, allowed us to complete more installations each day.

Other positions that you will eventually add to your team will include a lead stager, staging assistant, logistics manager, and possibly a marketing or social media professional.

GO ALL IN

Now that your business is up and running and you have systems, processes, and staff members, there are many affiliated organizations that you should become a part of:

- Local Business Networking – Look for organizations such as Business Networking International (BNI.com), where you can network with other business owners to get the word out about your company and services. This is part of your marketing expense but remember that people do business with those whom they know and respect, so get out and get known. Referrals are among the most productive sources of revenue for your company, so invest a portion of your time to generate referrals from the local business community.

- Local Real Estate Associations – Realtors are the primary source of business for staging companies. Make it your business to be very active and involved with all the real estate associations in your chosen market.
- Local Chamber of Commerce – Its entire reason for being is to help grow the interests of its members. Join and allow them to work on your behalf to assist you in promoting and growing your business.
- Home Builders Association – This is the association of local builders, craftsmen, and building contractors in your community. These are the people who build all the new homes in your market and are key customers for your business.
- Real Estate Staging Association – The industry's primary trade association dedicated to advancing professionalism and excellence in the industry. This is where you can learn from your peers and experts devoted to the industry.

As your business grows, your responsibilities as an owner begin to shift. You see your business plan come to life and your profit goals being met, and now, it's time to begin working *on* the business rather than *in* the business.

WORKING ON THE BUSINESS

"Generally speaking, it takes seven years to become an overnight success."
—Mike Dinsdale

Now that you have the right people on your bus, it's time to step back and begin working on the business rather than in the business. When you get to this point (which usually takes at least five years), you will need to take a good, long look at your current business plan. How has it changed? How have you changed? Where do you see yourself in the next year, two years, five years? Do you still love the business? Are your original bankers, lawyers, and accountants still the right fit for your organization? If not, it's time to interview some replacements. Have you been meeting your financial goals? More importantly, are you achieving the desired profit margins?

There is no set answer to any of the above questions. These tough questions and this type of analysis takes time and is not something that you can delegate to others. This is what I mean by working on the business.

Working on the business also means setting the direction and pace of the business. As the owner, you should devote time to forecasting business performance, personnel and training needs, investment needs, customer development and appreciation, etc. In effect, your business plan should become a living, forward-looking forecast encompassing a minimum of one, three, and five-year time horizons. This means you should be forecasting where you will be one year from now, three years from now, and five years from now. As you reach those appointed times, you should be grading yourself as the owner and resetting your forecast, making changes where necessary to allow you to reach your goals.

Once you have made it to the five-year mark (most small businesses fail within the first two years), you will have amassed a large amount of expertise in the home staging industry. You might want to consider another avenue like training other stagers, renting some of your existing inventory to other stagers, adding another service to your current business, or even getting out of the business altogether. Whichever avenue you choose, you will need to invest a significant amount of time and energy to implement your plans.

This is also a good time to begin performing an actual assessment or valuation of your company. A well-prepared and thorough report on your company is a huge asset for you as an owner. The assessment or valuation is more than an analysis of what your company is worth in the current market; it should also provide you with several key advantages:

- Gain an objective view of how productive the assets of your company are. Your business has working capital and investment needs, and the valuation will make clear what the state of your assets is and how they are performing for you and the business. This assessment can be vital in helping you make strategic business decisions, such as reinvesting all or a significant portion of your profits in additional assets or taking the money out for the benefit of the owners. You will also find these assessments are useful for you if you apply for a bank loan or take out additional insurance.
- Reveal weaknesses. An objective assessment of the company will illustrate areas of weakness in the performance and value of the business. This is very important for many reasons:
  o Nobody wants to fail, and if you are on a bad path, gaining the specific knowledge of the problem allows you to find expert help to correct your path.
  o Knowing where the weaknesses are, you can focus on them.
  o It takes time to overcome weakness and turn it into a neutral force or a strength. Since your objective as the owner is to build the maximum value into your business, knowing your weaknesses gives you time to fix them and turn them to your advantage.
- Benchmark your performance. As the owner, you are the only person in the business responsible for

the growth in value of the company. And if you don't measure it periodically, you will never know if you are building value, staying the same, or eroding value. A good practice is to make this assessment process as a recurring part of your business plan. Every three to five years, you should undergo this assessment and make sure you are always growing the value of your business.

- Be prepared for the worst. There are many inside and outside forces that can impact a business. Everything from the state of the economy to the medical emergency of a loved one will have an impact. When you are regularly assessing your strengths and weaknesses, you are better prepared to meet adversity when it inevitably happens.
- Prepare for retirement, a merger or acquisition, or the outright sale of the company. In all these instances, you want to know the financial impact your business will have on them. The assessment gives you that knowledge to assist in planning for retirement, thinking through how a merger or acquisition can benefit the company, or determining the range of value that the company may reasonably seek to achieve in a sale process.

If, at this point, you are considering selling your business, there are several steps you will need to take and a multitude of elements you will need to consider. Selling your business takes advance planning.

PART 2

Stage to Sell for the Highest Possible Amount

CHAPTER 6

ADVANCED PLANNING

"A good plan today is better than a perfect plan tomorrow."
–General George Patton

Up to this point, everything in this book can be considered advanced planning related to selling your home staging business. If you have followed the guidelines in the previous chapters, you should be in excellent shape as far as having the essential fundamentals in place to pursue selling your business. Early on, when you created your business plan, you asked yourself, *Will I have a family member working with me in the business? Will the family member want to take over the business when I leave? Will I have an employee who may want to buy the business?* Over the years, the answers to these questions should have become obvious, and you will have adjusted your business plan accordingly and will know which direction you will take in selling or winding down your business.

Before you even started your business, you should have had an idea of your exit strategy outlined in your business plan. Even if it was only a rough estimate, you would have continued to update your business plan and fleshed out your exit strategy as the years went by. It's important that you begin outlining your final exit plan **at least one year** prior to selling the business. If you are at the point that you don't want to wait a year (or can't afford to wait a year), you will need to diligently begin pulling your numbers together and set up a plan.

If you have decided to sell your business to a family member, it is vitally important that you work closely with your attorney and CPA. It is still beneficial to work with a business broker on the valuation of your company. When you initially meet your broker, you will need to let them know you are planning to sell to a family member. At this point, they will generally provide you with a fixed fee for providing the valuation and reviewing the sales agreement. At one point, I considered giving the company to my daughter since she had been working side-by-side with me since the beginning. Much to my dismay, I learned that you couldn't just give a business to someone, even your child. Once again, taxes come into play and in a big way. Always bring your CPA and attorney into the loop.

If you are the sole owner of your company, it makes it much easier to begin the process. If not, you will need to have frank and honest discussions with your business partners. Hopefully, you are all on the same page. In our case, I was the sole owner of the business, but my daughter was by my side and instrumental in growing the business and making all business decisions from day one.

TAX PLANNING

We all know there are two things that are certain in life: death and taxes. It is imperative that you bring your CPA and attorney into the loop when structuring the sale of your business. Did you know that an asset sale is taxed much more heavily than the part of the business applied to personal goodwill? Do you know the term *personal goodwill*? I didn't.

Over the years, I have seen many home stagers simply sell off their inventory and close their doors rather than sell their entire company. The backbone of your company—your employee manual, logo, website, social media, photos, trademarks, proprietary marketing materials, and client database—is much more valuable than the furnishings and is categorized as personal goodwill. Personal goodwill is taxed at a much lower rate than assets. Your business broker, attorney, and CPA will guide you in what percentage of the sale should be considered assets and what percentage applied to personal goodwill. This is a strategic plan that is different for every business.

An interesting fact that I learned in the sale of my business is that if the percentage of goodwill is higher and affects the seller favorably, it has the opposite effect on the buyer. It is a fine-line, give-and-take dance to develop numbers that are comfortable for both the seller and buyer. This is another area where your business broker and attorney play key roles in the negotiations. They handle all the negotiations with the buyer, so you don't have to.

CHAPTER 7

DECIDING TO SELL

*"The most difficult thing is the decision to act;
the rest is merely tenacity."*
—Amelia Earhart

Deciding to sell is often the most difficult part of the journey for those owners who dreamed up, started, and built their own business. The business is an extension of who they are and defines what they do each day and who they interact with. The act of making the decision to sell is often the most significant step on the path.

The decision to sell usually means that you have spent a lot of time thinking about who the perfect person will be to lead the business in the future. Owners often think of family, key employees, and competitors as they begin to go over the list of potential people in their minds. Many owners are very concerned about the legacy of the business and how the new leader will treat customers, employees, and suppliers. Selecting the right person to take the business into the future is a process that they think about in great detail. If the seller can't identify the right person, that's often a trigger that highlights for the seller that they will probably need help.

Several factors attributed to our decision to sell the business. One key consideration that I mentioned in the Introduction is the fact that my husband retired from his executive position of twenty-plus years. He was ready to relax and travel, and I was ready to go with him.

The next consideration was that my daughter and her family wanted to move to warm, sunny Florida, where we had vacationed for many years. While we relocated numerous times throughout her youth, she wanted to provide a lifelong residency and school and social environment for her daughter. A year before we decided to sell the company, the entire family took a trip to Florida to compare the various schools and communities. We even brought along our resident educational specialist, my husband's sister, to assist in assessing the schools. We all agreed on a school, and my granddaughter was accepted. This was in May 2018. We decided that we would make the move after the 2019 school year was complete.

In early June, we met for an informational session with a business broker, Steven Denny of Innovative Business Advisors. Steve was able to answer common seller questions like:

- Why should I use a broker?
- What type of businesses sell?
- How long does it take?
- What is the process really like?

- How do I keep employees/customers/suppliers from knowing?
- Should I offer to provide financing?
- What does it cost?

The key reasons for utilizing a business broker are as follows:

- The broker represents the seller's interests.
- Pricing is tricky, and valuation is critical. A good broker knows how to communicate the valuation.
- A broker knows the sale process and how to manage the process, including:
  o How to effectively analyze a business
  o How to obtain prequalification and financing for buyers
  o How to prepare an offer to purchase and other pertinent documents
  o How to handle due diligence, particularly managing contingencies and deadlines
  o How to handle the closing to ensure property conveyance

Statistics show that 99 percent of inquiries will not make an offer on a business. In most cases, it's like having an open house that never ends with an offer. A business broker knows how to handle all inquiries and won't waste your time with people who won't buy your business. Like a professional real estate agent, they get more deals closed.

As far as what type of businesses sell, Steve advised that saleable businesses all have three key traits:

- Good business track record with positive trends over an extended period
- Good financial records, including operating statements and tax returns
- Business offered at a fair market price that is justified with valuation

The entire process can take months to years, depending on the particulars of your business and your market. But don't be scared by that; most business sales happen within a six to twelve-month time frame.

AVOIDING SELLER'S REMORSE

Once the decision is made, what sellers often overlook is thinking about what they will do after the transaction is complete. It's quite common for sellers to spend a lot of time and effort coming to the decision but very little time thinking about the personal impact the transition will have on them. If you haven't put any thought into this, please do so before you move forward. Think of this as your Day One Plan, which is what you will do on the first day after you sign the closing papers and hand over the keys to the new owner. Studies have shown that sellers who don't have a solid plan for the next chapter of their lives often find themselves disappointed less than a year after the sale. What a tragedy it would be if you had time and money and ultimately came away with disappointment.

You grew your business from the ground up. You nurtured, you watered, you pruned, and finally, it blossomed. You sacrificed by working long hours and plowing every extra dollar into the company. After many years you have achieved your financial goals and your dream of owning a successful home staging company. You may have had family members working alongside you. You have certainly developed some wonderful business relationships and even long-term friendships with your agents and clients.

TRANSFERRING THE BUSINESS TO YOUR CHILD

One area of buyer's remorse that I haven't personally experienced, but has been shared with me, is when a family business has been transferred from parent to child and expectations haven't been met. This can happen for many reasons, from differences in generational values to differences in motivation. But the main cause is a lack of communication. In most cases, each party—parent and child—go into the succession process with either a different understanding about the correct approach for shifting leadership responsibilities or about what the business should be and how it should be run. Too often, these ideas are not discussed prior to the transition and inevitably cause both emotional and business stress for both parties.

To ensure the successful transference of the business from one generation to another, there are experiential differences between generations that must be considered. In many cases, the head of a family business is the one who built the business. Their experience—building something from scratch, working day and night to achieve success at the expense of a social life—is what they believe to be the recipe for success, and that recipe is what they expect from their children.

But that's rarely the case. The children have lived a far different life and often have financially benefited from the success of the family business, which makes their lives and their priorities very different. I have seen parents erroneously conclude that these differences equate to a lack of work ethic in the younger generation. These distinct life experiences can also create different ideas about how to approach the business, and in many cases, the desires of the next generation do not match up with the desires of the parent. This is when problems occur.

Many family business leaders have spent their lives building something that they want to pass on to their children, only to see that excitement turn to disappointment, dismay, feeling unappreciated, and even resentment. These disagreements and disappointments often leave parents and children in an uncomfortable stalemate. But the truth is, they are easy to avoid through communication—and a clear succession plan.

It's important to have honest conversations about compensation, timelines for transition, roles, and expectations years before you are ready to hand your business over to the next generation. Expectations must be laid out clearly, so when opinions and styles differ, they can be worked out long before the transition is made. Make yourself clear, but also be willing to listen. Just because you approach business one way, it doesn't mean it's the only way to achieve success. The world is changing, and the next generation might have ideas that will help drive business success after you depart.

Those who start family businesses are usually strong people who took a lot of risks to achieve success. It can come as a big surprise to some family business leaders that their offspring's style is very different from theirs, but that doesn't mean it won't work. In some cases, their style can be a big hit with clients and staff members. For instance, it might represent a welcome change to move from an emotional, passionate, frantic CEO to one who is calm, thoughtful, and never panics. What should never be lost are the aspects of style that have made the business successful—non-negotiable things like responsiveness and quality control.

Don't give away the business; sell it. Your child could experience major taxation should you simply gift the business to her. Many family business owners sell the business to their children, but at a price much lower than it would go for on the open market. It is important to outline the plan with your CPA well in advance.

Again, it is vitally important to have a business succession plan as part of your original business plan. The plan should include clear goals and benchmarks. It should include learning the business inside and out. If selling to your child, you might even plan to bring in an interim CEO to give her time to prepare to take over. The bottom line is to do everything possible to set your child (or any new owner of your business) up for success.

THE PATH TO SELLING YOUR STAGING BUSINESS

*"If you can find a path with no obstacles,
it probably doesn't lead anywhere."*
—Frank A. Clark

Selling your staging business for the highest amount possible is a team effort. You must take time to carefully interview the team who will assist in the sale of your business, similar to hiring employees. As we have discussed previously, a business broker is one of the most important team members. Do your research, ask around, check references, and find the broker who best fits your needs. Our broker helped us assemble the rest of the team required to successfully sell the company. Our team consisted of our broker, an attorney, and our accountant.

Once you have decided on a broker, you will be provided with an Exclusive Sales Listing Agreement. In my case, it was a seven-page document with five exhibits. This agreement will outline the services to be provided by the broker, the broker's compensation schedule, seller obligations, and other general legalese. Most brokers utilize a standard listing agreement. Be sure to read it carefully and have it reviewed by your attorney. Nothing is set in stone. Your attorney may suggest some modifications to the original agreement. Now that you have come to terms with the agreement, it's time to get to work.

Working with a broker is a sound investment. Your broker will offer you professionalism, complete confidentiality, comprehensive marketing, and a defined conveyance process. Generally, a broker will require a retainer to begin the process and, depending on the valuation of the business, a set fee or a percent of the sale price of the business. The broker is generally paid at the closing table.

Selecting the right attorney is as important as selecting the right broker to market your business. Your broker should be an excellent resource to provide you with multiple referrals for an attorney who specializes in the sale of small businesses. There are a multitude of intricacies involved in the sale of a business, and you want an attorney who is proficient and up to date in this area. Brian Rogers of Blue Maven Law LLC did an excellent job assisting us in navigating the sale of the business. Prior to signing a Letter of Engagement, you will want to discuss the attorney's fees relating to the sale of the business. The attorney may offer a flat fee for handling all aspects of the sale or a combination of a flat fee and an hourly rate for unexpected incidentals. It's important to know what to expect before you receive the first invoice. In our case, we provided a retainer up front and were billed at various stages throughout the process, which worked very well for our needs.

Prior to marketing your business, your attorney will assist you in determining the elements of your business that can be categorized as intellectual property. Your attorney will be of assistance throughout the process and after the sale.

Why is it important to have an attorney involved throughout the process? Because ultimately, they will save you more than they cost you. Let's say you hire an attorney to provide an opinion on a document. He or she will comment on the lawfulness and accuracy of it. This type of transaction contractor won't advocate for your benefit or help you structure the document for your particular advantage. They won't know all the circumstances surrounding the transaction and won't be privy to the motivations and objectives of the parties. They'll have a very limited view of the transaction and will only comment on the particulars in front of them. Therefore, they might not be in sync with what you want to achieve. Thus, you end up paying for a legal opinion that is accurate and lawful but may not be the best way to handle the circumstance to your advantage.

This is entirely different from engaging an attorney as part of an assembled team at the start of the selling process. When an attorney is engaged from the beginning, they'll be able to advocate for your overall goal. They'll draft, review, and negotiate terms with only you in mind.

If you have reached the point in your business where you are actively pursuing selling it, you probably have an ongoing relationship with an excellent accountant. You will recall that accounting was discussed at length in Chapter 3. You should be able to generate required financial reports directly from QuickBooks or whatever financial accounting system your business uses. However, many lenders require reports generated through your CPA or even audited financial reports.

Your accountant or CPA will also be instrumental in assisting in the structuring of the sale as far as assets and personal goodwill as they relate to your overall tax picture. Your CPA may suggest that rather than being paid the entire sale amount up front, that you have payments structured in increments over a period. Your CPA may suggest, based on your tax situation, that you offer owner financing of the business. Once again, it pays off handsomely to work with a team of professionals throughout the entire process of selling the business.

Teams always protect the interest of the party they represent. They pay attention to the details and make sure they achieve the best possible outcome for their side of the transaction. Buyers often have an assembled team. If you choose to represent yourself as the seller, you might find that you're sitting alone, across the table from the buyer and their full team. The buyer's team will always want to control the deal timing and the document production because it gives them the best chance to get what they want out of the transaction. While they may consider your requests, their intent is to structure the transaction in a way that benefits them as buyers. This puts the solo seller at a disadvantage and can lead to giving up terms and conditions that have significant impacts.

Sellers may choose the DIY approach because hiring a team costs money, and they want to spend as little as possible to net larger proceeds. But what happens is often the opposite. When the buyer has a team, but a seller doesn't, the terms can be skewed toward the buyer, and the seller can end up losing more money than if they had invested in hiring a team.

For example, let's talk about an *earn-out*. That's when a buyer pays you for your business over time after the ownership has changed, based on the actual performance of the business as compared to the targeted performance of the business. Statistically, earn-outs are heavily weighted in the buyer's favor. You, as the seller, may agree to terms that appear reasonable during negotiation because they resemble what you've experienced up to that point. However, you don't have the experience of strategic thinking about potential future impact and thus can't imagine a situation where the deal won't work out as designed.

From the seller's perspective, an earn-out is often challenging because the seller will have no control over the business during the future period when the earn-out is paid. Thus, the seller must rely on the good faith of the buyer along with the achievement of the metric, which triggers the earn-out—areas that you have no control over. While an earn-out appears to favor the buyer, sellers have other alternatives such as owner financing, consulting agreements, or other contractual means to facilitate a transaction that works for the benefit of both buyer and seller.

The team is designed to give you a superior return, often realized in less time spent negotiating and superior deal terms. Your team will have a strategy and will have predetermined what's in your best interest.

A superior return will factor in the tax impact of the deal. Ultimately, what really matters is how much you get to keep after all expenses and taxes. Your team will maximize that amount and accomplish the goal.

It's not hard to assemble your team. Talk to your current advisors (accountants, bankers, attorneys) and ask if they have experience in the transaction process. If they have little or no experience, then ask them for referrals to those who do have experience. The key is to gather folks together who specialize in the transaction process. Set an introductory meeting with these new referrals to review their experience and competence and to determine if you'd enjoy working with them.

GATHERING DETAILS FOR THE TEAM

Many factors come into play when selling your small business. Your broker will require the following documents and information to be utilized in compiling the valuation of your company.

- Three years of financial statements either CPA compiled or audited
    - o Income and expense summary
    - o Balance sheet
    - o Tax returns
    - o Current quarter-end income and expense summary and balance sheet
- Copy of all leases
- Copy of all employment contracts

- Depreciation schedule of all equipment
- Current accounts receivable aging report
- Current accounts payable aging report
- Employee benefits packages and employee manual
- List of equipment including valuation
- Copy of all business licenses
- Copy of LLC incorporation papers, articles of association, and bylaws
- Name of attorney
- Name of CPA
- Listing of all personal withdrawals, benefits, auto, or personal expenses in company income and expense reports
- Pending lawsuits

Note, your broker will need all this information before he can begin compiling your business valuation. That is why it is so critical to set up the proper processes and procedures and relationships with a strong CPA and attorney before you even start business operations.

Your broker will also ask you to provide the following:

- Executive summary
- Business overview
    - o Business essentials (address, phone, fax)
    - o Owner information/primary contact
- Business data
    - o Company's legal entity
    - o Company's DBA
    - o Years established/years owned
    - o State of incorporation
    - o Date of incorporation

- o Company legal status
- o Business category
- o Primary SIC code (the business activity code off your tax returns)
- o Years at current location
- o Company employee information
- Management and ownership
  - o Number of hours owner works per week
  - o Common shares outstanding
  - o Share price
  - o Functions the seller currently performs
  - o Roster of key positions and summary of responsibilities
  - o Does the owner want to continue to work in the business?
  - o Why is the owner selling the business?
  - o Number of family members working in the business and their positions
- Marketing and distribution
  - o Primary target market
  - o Market trends for company's product
  - o How the company markets
  - o Description of company's services
  - o List of patents, copyrights, or trademarks
  - o Cyclical factors to consider regarding this service impacting sales or profitability
  - o How the company sells and distributes the services
- Customer information
  - o General overview of company's customer base

- o Potential customers to market to or growth areas that the buyer could implement to increase business
- o Tips and advice to the buyer based on past experience
- Full list of competitors
- Projections on how many months an individual with reasonable skills and little direct knowledge of the business would need to learn enough about the business to manage it properly
- Skills or licenses required to operate the business

If you have been maintaining comprehensive records related to your business, the process of compiling this information will be fairly straightforward. If not, you will have to invest hours into pulling it together before your broker can begin the process. Once your broker has this information, he will complete the business valuation.

Our business advisor (Steve Denny of Innovative Business Advisors) took the process a step further. His company utilizes a proprietary process called the Value Builder System™. This is a thirteen-page questionnaire relating to your industry, your customers, your staff, future projections, and other facts and figures. This is especially important for a new industry like home staging as most brokers have never endeavored to sell a home staging business. Knowledge is power. The more your broker knows about you and your industry, the better prepared he will be to "sell" potential buyers.

A tool that some advisors utilize is a TTM (trailing twelve months) performance checkup. This provides a snapshot of the business but does not go as in-depth as the Value Builder System. This is the program that our CPA utilized in determining a value for our business, and as stated earlier, that valuation was less than half the amount we ended up receiving for our business through the retention of a qualified and experienced business broker.

Another key reason for working with a business broker is that you, the owner, can continue to maintain focus on successfully operating the business while they focus on putting all the materials together, marketing the business, and getting it closed. Rest assured, the lender will be checking your numbers right up until the closing of the sale.

OBJECTIVE BUSINESS ASSESSMENT

When you have the team in place, it's time to do an objective business assessment. As noted above, our business broker prepared a comprehensive, copyrighted Value Builder Report as the first step in the process. This provided us with a twenty-eight-page document that analyzed eight key value builder drivers of our business, including:

1. Financial Performance – What is the sales volume, gross profit, earnings before interest, taxes, depreciation and amortization, the net operating profits, and the amount of money the owners pay themselves? These key measures of financial performance are considered the cornerstone of business valuation.
2. Growth Value – The potential for growth can be a key value driver for certain buyer types. In the financial calculations noted above, this could be reflected in the discounted value of future earnings. Imagine

a business that is on the cusp of releasing a new product or beginning to serve a new contract. The future revenue growth of the business is forecast to be impacted by 20 percent or more, a percentage of growth realized by less than 2 percent of American companies. This strong amount of growth is a key value driver for strategic buyers and should therefore be accounted for in the worth calculation of the business.

3. Dependence/The Switzerland Structure – Is the business overly dependent on any one customer, employee, or supplier? If so, this negatively impacts its value because buyers are concerned about the real risk of that loss. The opposite of this is a business that isn't dependent on any one customer, employee, or supplier. There's little to no risk if a single customer is lost. There's also minimal risk with a business that has a strong training process and can quickly replace any employee. The same is true of a business that can source material at comparable prices from a wide variety of suppliers. In each of these instances, a business that experiences little to no impact from a change in customer, employee, or supplier is much more stable and less risky than a business dependent on one or more of these factors.

4. Valuation Teeter-Totter – This measures the impact of cash flow, gross margin, and profitability on the value of a business. It refers to the relationship between working capital and earnings. If your working capital grows out of proportion to the cash generated by the business, then a buyer won't be willing to pay

more for the earnings because they'll need to write an additional (and potentially bigger) check for the working capital. If a business generates cash as it grows and requires little additional working capital because the business funds its own expansion, then a buyer is likely to pay more for the earnings.

5. Recurring Revenue – How is the sales revenue generated? This is one of the primary areas of interest for a buyer. If a business has a high degree of recurring customers or a business model that relies on regular, recurring subscription-type payments from its customers, then it's easy for a buyer to value the future stream of revenue. If a business must go out and hunt new customers month after month and has little or no recurring revenue from its existing customers, then its future stream of revenue is harder to value and has a higher risk associated with it. High risk always leads to a discount in value. Highly reliable revenue streams lead to low risk and an increase in value.

6. Monopoly Control – This dimension of value measures the uniqueness of a business. A unique business is difficult for competitors to duplicate and, therefore, earns a premium measure in this area. If a business is commoditized and easily duplicated in the marketplace, then the business value is reduced. This differentiation from the competition makes a particular business opportunity unique and meaningful. Strategic buyers often seek out these types of businesses for acquisition.

7. Customer Satisfaction – This dimension measures both the extent to which customers are satisfied as

well as a business's ability to assess customer satisfaction in a consistent and rigorous way. Satisfied customers often equate to loyal customers, and loyal customers deliver referrals and recurring revenue. A business that proactively measures customer satisfaction and can demonstrate that it has a system and process of growing satisfaction over time is more valuable to a buyer than a comparable business with no measurement or control system.

8. Hub & Spoke – This measures how dependent the business is on the owner's efforts within it. If the owner is the center of all functions, the business will enter a phase of high risk when the owner steps away. On the other hand, if a business can succeed and grow with little to no impact from the owner's absence, then the business risk is low for a potential buyer. Many buyers fear what impact an ownership change will have on a business. If the impact is little to none, then a buyer will place a higher value on the business.

Each of these key value-builder drivers is scored, and your company is given an overall score, all of which are also compared to the industry average. This is another key component in assessing many aspects of your business, which becomes a part of establishing the estimate of fair market value of your company.

> **Would you like to know how your business scores on the Value Builder Assessment?**

> *If so, please apply to join our Facebook Private Group "Selling Your Staging Business," then request the link to the questionnaire, and we will be happy to provide it to you FREE of charge (normally $500)!*

Our broker also provided a Business Bankability Method™ valuation analysis. The Bankability Method is used to analyze and measure the demonstrated cash production capability of the business. Since traditional bank lending is the most common form of credit for businesses generating less than $10 million in annual revenue, it's relevant to use a valuation method that answers the questions:

- What is a bank willing to lend to a credit-worthy borrower who wants to purchase an existing business of this type?
- How will the bank come to that lending dollar amount conclusion?

Determining the amount of cash flow that the business produces allowed us to calculate the amount of debt coverage that the business can service from its demonstrated cash flow. From that amount of debt coverage, we could then calculate a debt service coverage ratio that measures the ratio of cash flow available to service each dollar of debt coverage. This key ratio is used by lenders to determine if there is ample cash to cover any proposed debt payments associated with a loan to purchase the business.

Finally, the report illustrated a calculation of equity injection (down payment) and interest rate that is commensurate with the current market rates. The result is a bankable value (i.e., the price a credit-worthy buyer can pay that is financeable for the company). The report calls this "Bankability Method – Estimated Selling Price."

In our case, this turned out to be an important measure of the value as the buyer did purchase our staging business using a bank loan, and our calculations were instrumental in the buyer getting financing. All of this ties together to provide potential buyers with a sense of security and reassurance that the asking price of the business is a fair one.

Once your broker has provided you with the fair market value range for your business, you can decide if you still want to move forward with the sale of your business. Your broker will tell you honestly if he feels there is truly a market for your business at this time or in the future. The valuation may not be what you expect. Your broker will walk you through exactly how he came up with the valuation. The numbers don't lie, and any savvy buyer will be able to look at the numbers and know if they are on target. If you decide to move forward, your broker will prepare the marketing campaign, a list of potential target buyers, and a complete package of business opportunity documents to be provided to potential buyers.

Your business is worth the total of what you own minus what you owe plus the processes and systems, inventory, and cash flow generation capability of your business. Inventory is a tangible asset that is valued in the sale process, but the quality of your customers, the quality of your systems, and the quality of your cash flow are intangibles. Those intangibles all roll up into the personal goodwill factor. That is what makes up the big difference in valuation between one company and another.

In essence, you could have two million-dollar staging companies that are in the same town and doing basically the same level of revenue. If one is essentially a seat-of-the-pants operation that has no processes or formal systems in place, but they're pretty good salespeople, really good hustlers, and they go out and get the job done, sometimes by hook or crook or whatever, then that business will be valued at a much lower level than a business like ours that had great people, great processes, and everything very well organized. Our business operated independently of the owner because of the systems and processes that were firmly in place. If a business runs just as smoothly when the owner is away on vacation with her family, then that is a business not dependent on the owner and will be worth a premium in comparison to another business without that key trait. A business like that would have a much higher level of goodwill in it and a much higher value, even though the revenues of the business look to be identical.

DOCUMENTS AND EXHIBITS

We provided a lot of documents and information to our broker, and they came back to us with a recommended selling price that we were excited about. The next steps involved working with our team to assemble the informational documents used to market our business. Our broker had a well-defined set of steps to walk us through the process:

- First meeting – The broker determines if the owner and the business are ready to sell. After this meeting, a valuation meeting will be scheduled.
- Second meeting – Business review
    - This is an in-depth business review of the process and agreements.
    - During this meeting, the broker will also review data requirements, which the business owner will have to assemble (noted above).
    - Review the business valuation documents and determine if the price range is acceptable to the seller
- Third through Fifth Meetings – Review the representations
- Marketing begins – Collect and accept offer(s)
- Offer is accepted – Due diligence process begins
    - Potential buyer gets all questions answered.
    - Financing is arranged and committed
    - Final purchase agreement terms are agreed upon
- Final step – Closing and conveyance

There are several steps to the closing process, including:

- Meeting with employees after closing to introduce new owner
- Meeting with customers to introduce new owner
- Seller provided buyer training after closing

One of the most important elements involved in selling your business is keeping it confidential. Using a business broker is the best way to assure confidentiality. The business name and location (other than the city and state) are not included in the marketing materials. Before receiving any additional information other than the marketing requirements, prospective buyers must sign a confidentiality agreement. All meetings relating to the sale of the business are conducted in the broker's office or another location off-site.

CHAPTER 9

THE INFORMATIONAL DOCUMENTS

"As we start looking for the good, our focus automatically is taken off the bad."
—Susan Jeffers

Your broker will immediately begin creating a marketing package that will be provided to prequalified potential buyers. This marketing package will include a professional marketing piece that lists your company's competitive advantages, markets served, awards and designations, as well as photos of your business offices, warehouse space, vehicles, and overall inventory.

Prior to providing these marketing materials, potential buyers will receive a confidential packet of information relating to the business. In our case, these were referred to as business opportunity documents. Your company name and contact information are not included on these materials. Page one includes a notification that this is a confidential memorandum relating to a client of your business advisor. The second page is a notice of confidentiality. The prospective buyer must read and sign a confidentiality agreement prior to receiving this package. This page also outlines their obligation of non-disclosure and that the person reviewing the package will be held liable for the confidentiality of the material provided.

This packet will also include financial statements. As mentioned, your company name is not provided on the materials; however, a savvy competitor or client may readily recognize that it is your firm. That is why confidentiality is so important and why your broker has taken the time to evaluate the financial capability of the prospective buyer.

CONFIDENTIALITY

Most businesses don't hang a FOR SALE sign when the owner is ready to move on. You probably don't want your current customers, employees, and suppliers to be aware of the transaction process until it's complete. You also don't want a prospective buyer talking about the business being for sale within their industry or in your market. For these reasons and more, it's standard practice to first share a non-disclosure agreement (NDA) with a potential buyer.

An NDA determines who a potential buyer can talk to regarding the details of the business for sale. It's an enforceable agreement and has some teeth, and it is designed to underscore the serious damage that can occur if the parties don't honor the agreement. Experienced brokers and advisors will come prepared to customize a template agreement to match your needs as the seller.

The Informational Documents

There are numerous reasons for extreme caution and confidentiality at this point in the process.

- Your competition could get wind of the sale and reach out to your current clients to obtain their business.
- Your employees could learn of the sale and become anxious and seek other employment.
- Your outside vendors or resources could reach out to competitive stagers if they fear you will not be providing them with as much business.

Confidentiality is even more critical when it comes to your competitors and current clients getting wind of the sale of your company. The last thing you want to happen during the sales process is for your current clients to begin hearing rumors through the grapevine. A confidentiality leak can leave your business very vulnerable to your competition.

For example, you may have a competitor who has been trying for months to make inroads with one of your key clients. This competitor contacts your client and plants the bug in their ear that you are selling your business, or worse yet, indicates that you may be going out of business. The competitor then offers to step in and offer their staging services. Your customers may feel slighted that you hadn't contacted them, and without even having a conversation with you, move on to utilizing the services of the competitor. You definitely want to control the narrative.

There is always a chance that confidentiality could be breached, or a competitor or other industry professional gets wind of the potential sale. If employees begin asking pointed questions, try to be as vague as possible, but at the same time, reassuring.

This happened during the process of selling our business. A team member heard something and shared it with two other employees. One of the employees came to me and asked for confirmation. Before providing any information, I quickly called the entire team together so that everyone would receive the same information at the same time. The sales agreement that was drawn up by my attorney provided a clause that all our existing employees would retain their current (or higher) positions and salary and benefits for a period of at least one year. Without providing the name of the individual purchasing the company, I assured my team that the individual was a strong businessperson, financially solvent, and intended to continue growing the business. Even with these assurances, some team members became extremely nervous. It was a hand-holding process once the proverbial cat was out of the bag. The bottom line is to keep it on the down-low for as long as possible.

After a potential buyer agrees and signs the NDA, they'll receive information that identifies your specific business and its operating characteristics. This information will often include a summary document known as a flyer or brochure. This document will be concise and have one or more pertinent facts designed to entice the buyer to seek additional information. It will focus on benefits and will position the business in the best possible light.

INFORMATIONAL DOCUMENTS

When planning to sell your business, be prepared for a six to twelve-month timeline. The more time you spend planning and preparing for the sale of your business, the better chance you have of selling your business for the price you are seeking. Only after an interested party has accepted and signed the terms of confidentiality, the following documents are shared:

TEASER / FLYER / BROCHURE

The broker compiles all the information, facts, figures, and photos you have provided and creates marketing materials that will effectively showcase the business to potential buyers. A professional business broker has firsthand knowledge of what information is most important in marketing your business. The broker effectively extrapolates the information in an informative and concise manner that showcases the most attractive elements of the business.

CONFIDENTIAL INFORMATION MEMORANDUM (CIM)

This is one of the most comprehensive documents that your broker will prepare. It's designed to be an executive summary of your business and will touch on each of the eight main characteristics covered in the assessment document. This document is objective by design. It highlights the strengths of the business, which provides the prospective buyer with a solid overview of the opportunity.

The CIM includes many business-specific summaries, including those of the financial statements, business system, and process overviews. These documents provide a comprehensive view of what happens both publicly and behind the scenes of your company. They provide a lot of information but don't include any trade secrets or special proprietary information that could give a competitor a strategic advantage. The goal is to provide the prospective buyer with enough information for them to deliver a formal response indicating their interest in acquiring your business.

Many times, a prospective buyer will review the CIM and then ask for supporting documents to help them understand more about a specific aspect of the business. For example, they may want to understand how dependent the business is on its customers, so they might ask for a list of customers ranked by the proportion of sales revenue each customer represents.

These supporting documents are normal and customary but must be prepared in a way that will satisfy the buyer without divulging trade secrets, including customer names. It is appropriate to share additional details to get to a deal, but most of this type of activity occurs during the diligence period. These documents form the foundation of the marketing packet, and there will be additional documents developed to highlight specific aspects of the business and contemplated transaction.

When all the informational documents are complete, the next step is to set the ideal buyer target by developing the ideal buyer profile. In building the profile, the goal is to answer the following question: Who will pay the most because they'll get the biggest benefit from acquiring this business?

The Informational Documents

Often the answer is a strategic buyer—a buyer who can gain market share, product range, additional location, or another aspect complementary to their existing business. Occasionally, one might target a technical expert, a craftsperson, or other lifestyle buyer who may generate the highest value by achieving a specific individual objective. But in all instances, you want to make sure the marketing plan and informational documents speak to the financial buyer, the buyer whose first consideration is the investment characteristics of the business opportunity.

Once your team has an ideal buyer profile, the broker will disseminate the information to his vast network of contacts as well as to the contacts you have identified. This is not a shotgun approach to marketing but rather a targeted list of potential buyers. One of the most delicate aspects of selling the business is maintaining seller confidentiality throughout the initial process, which leads us to the next step in the sales process. Then it's simply a matter of reaching out to them and engaging them in a dialogue to determine who's interested and capable of buying the business.

CHAPTER 10

CHOOSE YOUR SUCCESSOR

"You can tell whether a man is clever by his answers. You can tell whether a man is wise by his questions."
—Naguib Mahfouz

You might be wondering who would buy your business. The answer is that it depends. It depends on the nature of the business and how it's performing. For simplicity's sake, think in terms of three types of buyers:

1. Lifestyle or entrepreneurial buyers
2. Economic buyers
3. Strategic buyers

These buyer types can be individuals or companies. Motivations vary from type to type, and the ideal business fit is different for each buyer. The buyer's motivations are key to understanding how to engage with them. It also helps to understand what they value most in a transaction and how they'll gauge the offer price in relation to what they're willing to pay.

Motivations vary from type to type, and the ideal business fit is different for each buyer.

1. LIFESTYLE OR ENTREPRENEURIAL BUYERS

The lifestyle buyer makes up the largest pool of available buyers in any market. Typically, a lifestyle buyer is an individual person, and these buyers represent the bulk of inbound inquiries from an advertisement for a business opportunity. Generally speaking, these buyers want to work for themselves, they have some money saved, and they're seeking an ideal opportunity. As the world becomes more connected, people from every corner of the globe have access to see and respond to opportunities to acquire businesses.

Their specific motivations may vary, but these people are looking for an opportunity to work without having to report to a boss. And yet, when I talk to them, I often find they don't have any actual experience working for themselves. It's the idea of working for themselves that they find so compelling.

Generally, lifestyle buyers set their sights on their own experiences. Thus, if they currently make $50,000 per year, they seek a business opportunity that allows them to make a low multiple of that—perhaps $150,000 per year. They think that the answer to their prayers will be having a multiple of their current earnings plus the freedom to work for themselves.

Ultimately, this vision provides them the lifestyle of their dreams. That's why I refer to them as lifestyle buyers; they seek to find a business opportunity that will give them the lifestyle they desire.

The entrepreneurial buyer is a variation of this buyer type. Like the lifestyle buyer, their scope and vision are restricted to their experience. However, they often have the added dimension of working for another company in the same industry. Because of this experience, they usually have the strong belief that they have the entrepreneurial drive to do the job better than the company they work for. These buyers have some savings or equity they can access, and if they find the right opportunity, they know they can innovate something compelling and prosper.

There's another variation on this same theme—the technical expert or craftsman buyer. Like the others, they have a limited scope and ability, but they also have a deep knowledge or skill set that differentiates them. Again, they seek an opportunity where they can work without a boss.

Individuals in this buyer classification do buy businesses. But they do so infrequently and rarely more than once. They have money to spend and can make time around their work and life schedule to investigate opportunities, but they have a hard time finding the right opportunity. They're the window shoppers of the transaction universe and will spend a tremendous amount of time following their dream of how a process should work, but they have little knowledge or experience completing transactions.

2. ECONOMIC BUYERS

There has been explosive growth in this category of buyers. They can be either private individuals or entities, and they have the money to buy. They generally fall into three subcategories and are all motivated by the opportunity to put their money (or fund money) to work to generate a return.

The explosive growth in this category has come from the recent development of the first subcategory of financial buyers known as *private equity*. These entities are made up of partners and managers. The partners are individuals with money and expertise in a particular business or industry. The partners pool their money, leverage their expertise and contacts, and seek to accelerate the growth of a company, thereby multiplying the enterprise value of the company they acquire. The partners deploy managers to oversee the businesses day to day, and they add investment capital to generate economies of scale by using similar systems and processes across their organization. As of this writing, it's estimated that there are more than 10,000 entities of this type in the United States, and that number is growing.

If a private equity organization has raised a fund of capital to invest, then they'll have a particular period in which to put their capital to work and a specific period to hold the entities they acquire. Generally, private equity companies buy and hold a company for five to seven years, then sell it with the goal of realizing a minimum predetermined return on their capital. Funds within these entities are quite specific in their investment criteria and quickly determine whether or not a deal meets these criteria.

These buyers are often very astute and have an experienced transaction team. Transactions are their focus (both buying and selling), with a hold period in between. These experienced teams often overwhelm business owners. Private equity entities evaluate many opportunities and grow bored or pass on an opportunity that might be ideal for them if the seller can't produce information on their timetable and format.

Private equity buyers are extremely transparent about their motivations. Buyers in this field even advertise the ideal fit for them and describe it in terms of the business operation and the financial performance desired. Private equity buyers may even have salespeople working for them who actively solicit other transaction professionals and use sophisticated tools to surface ideal candidates for them.

The second subcategory is known as *private investment*. Warren Buffet is the poster child for this type of entity. He uses his original company, Berkshire Hathaway, as a means to purchase particular businesses. Unlike private equity companies, private investment companies often invest money attributed to one specific entity or individual (versus pooling funds), and private investment buyers also purchase with the intention to hold or own indefinitely. Private equity must sell at some point in the future, but private investment has no such mandate.

Both buyer types are also similar in certain ways. Both openly discuss their motivation for purchase, and both closely evaluate the opportunity based on financial return. The private investment entity may have different return criteria but are often open and transparent about what they expect. A big difference is that private investment buyers don't use debt to purchase a business—they don't borrow funds. Buyers of this type typically purchase on a cash basis and want to own one hundred percent of a company.

They're also very astute buyers. They evaluate hundreds of opportunities and invest in relatively few. They look for a specific set of criteria and won't waste your time window-shopping the deal. They'll respond promptly and will make offers and close deals as quickly as possible.

The third subcategory is the *private investor*. This is typically a private individual who invests their own personal money. Their motivation is similar to the others, and they primarily buy and hold a business. Investors of this type typically pay cash and like to own one hundred percent of the entity they acquire. The primary difference here is that they may only hold a single entity at a time—not multiple companies.

All three of these types of buyers typically focus on companies with EBITDA (earnings before interest, taxes, depreciation, and amortization) annual cashflows of greater than $1 million and normally won't consider smaller companies.

3. STRATEGIC BUYERS

This type of buyer can be an individual or a company. Strategic buyers are interested in purchasing for a specific outcome that will enhance their current business. Strategic buyers often stretch and pay more than a financial or lifestyle buyer because, typically, they'll receive an immediate and outsized benefit from the purchase.

Their motivations can be any of the following:

- Add a complementary or line extension to their product portfolio
- Add a location
- Add a range of products or services
- Add sales capability
- Eliminate a competitor from the marketplace
- Add technology or capability
- Remove or reduce fixed or variable cost

And this only begins to explain their motivations. In general, the combination of what strategic buyers already have plus the opportunity the seller provides equals more than they can build on their own. It's a 1+1= >2 equation.

Strategic buyers are often experienced at acquisitions and may follow a specific formula. They generally have a team of transaction experts and will move quickly to get a transaction done. They're often motivated to act and close before competitors or peers in the market have the opportunity.

IDEAL BUYER

Your broker will assist you in determining your ideal buyer. Prior to engaging your broker, you may have come up with a list of possible purchasers for your business. Be sure that you shared this with your broker and that it was addressed in the exclusive sales listing agreement. If one of these candidates ends up purchasing your business, your compensation to the broker will be much less than if he secures a buyer due to his marketing efforts. Potential buyers for your business could include current competition, current customers, or investors (as noted above).

- **Current competition.** You will have provided your broker with a list of your current competitors as part of the questionnaire discovery process. You will be able to guide him on which competitors you feel would be likely candidates interested in purchasing your company. You can also instruct your broker on competitors you do not wish to have contacted regarding the sale of the business.
- **Current customers.** Your best customers may be ideal candidates interested in purchasing your business. It may be a perfect fit for one of your key homebuilding clients or real estate flippers or investors. These clients generally have access to the capital needed to purchase a business and the tax incentive to do so.
- **Investors.** There are many individuals who need a place to invest their cash. These folks may not have anything to do with the staging industry, or they may have a business that is ancillary to home staging. This could be a perfect fit for their business plan. Your broker will have the contacts and know how to flesh out these types of potential buyers.

For many sellers, the ideal buyer is the person or entity who will take the least amount of time in diligence, is prepared to pay the highest price in cash at closing, and won't change a thing concerning the business operation. An ideal buyer is rare and highly sought after. When it comes to identifying the ideal buyer, several attributes are clearly recognizable.

First is their ability to pay the asking price. It's normal and customary for potential buyers to exhibit their ability to pay either through their own resources or by demonstrating their borrowing capacity. Brokers and advisors will have a process in place where prospective buyers qualify themselves.

Another clearly recognizable attribute is industry experience or relevance. This is particularly important if a portion of the purchase price will be financed. Lenders look long and hard at experience when they qualify a buyer for lending. If SBA funding is contemplated, this attribute is required.

TARGET IDEAL BUYER MOTIVATION

The marketing message needs to speak to the motivation of the ideal buyer. The buyer seeks a certain something, so the seller's message should speak to that certain something. This core message should be part of all marketing elements. This is a secret sauce that brokers use to attract the right buyers.

The marketing elements include the headlines used in the advertising methods. A headline should shout to the ideal buyer and herald a single key feature of the opportunity. It should stop the buyer and get them to investigate further, to seek the additional details.

The additional details are also called *teaser data*. Teaser data includes up to five key benefits the opportunity represents and provides basic financial information like annual gross revenue and some measurement of profit and cash flow. This information allows the browsing buyer to quickly identify if the opportunity fits their criteria.

At that point, the prospective buyer may request additional information, which opens the door for you to learn about the buyer.

BUSINESS BUYER'S PACKAGE

Your broker will provide you with a list of potential buyer contacts for your approval prior to launching the marketing plan. He will follow up with contacts, field questions, and provide information. You will not be talking to potential buyers until near the end of the process.

Your broker should prepare a business buyer's package. One of the most important elements of this package is the buyer's personal profile or confidential information summary. The buyer provides personal information, experience, or skills that would be of benefit in owning the company, work history, background, and comprehensive financial information, including:

- Down payment dollars available and the source
- Summarized personal financial statement
    - o Assets
    - o Liabilities
    - o Net worth
    - o Other sources of income

If the buyer is interested and you are willing to offer seller financing, the broker will require tax returns and a credit report to be submitted along with the offer to purchase. If the buyer is interested in financing a purchase using a combination of cash or seller financing plus lender financing with or without Small Business Administration (SBA) underwriting, the broker will require your personal financial statement, tax returns, credit report, and resume for the loan application. The buyer will also need a down payment (equity injection) of 10–25% of the total project cost (purchase price plus fees) and other collateral acceptable to a lender. For SBA lending, the buyer will need to complete IRS Form 1919 and Form 413. Your broker will provide the buyer instructions for completing each of these forms.

IS IT NECESSARY FOR BUYERS TO WALK THROUGH THE BUSINESS?

Your employees, customers, and suppliers probably don't know your business is being marketed for sale. You may feel that if you let buyers walk through the business during normal business hours, it would put your business in jeopardy. But buyers want to see the business operating. They want to see how it performs in its normal course of action and to get a sense of how it's received by its customers and market.

This is an extremely tricky aspect of selling your business. Eventually, your broker will need to come to your business to preview and photograph the space and your inventory. Employees may begin asking, "Who is that person?" Once you have an interested buyer who has signed an offer to purchase, that person will want to preview the space and most likely bring their people along. All of these out-of-the-ordinary visits may raise even more questions. It is imperative that you carry on with business as usual for as long as possible. Even your most trusted employees can become nervous and apprehensive, which can affect the morale of your entire team. How do you resolve this?

Consider producing a pictorial of your business yourself, or hire a professional real estate photographer to come take photos and video of the business. While it still involves an outsider, if it is a real estate photographer known in your market, it may be easier to explain it. Once you have this, it will allow you to show the buyer a comprehensive view of the business without the buyer having to come out and physically inspect the business. You can arrange the photo shoot to minimize the impact on business operations.

These virtual tours achieve two key goals. One, they give the buyer a visual image of the business that satisfies their initial curiosity and ensures the business fits their criteria. Two, they enable you to have minimal disruption to your business operations during the sale process.

There will come a time when the buyer wants to visit the business before the sale is completed. But a wise seller won't want that to happen until well after the diligence process has begun. The site visit becomes a confirmation visit during the diligence process, not an interruption of your daily business operations. During the diligence stage, there may be several different types of inspections and visits that occur, and you'll have time to coordinate them appropriately.

BE PREPARED FOR IDEAL BUYER QUESTIONS

The most commonly asked question is, "Why are you for sale?" or "If your business is so great, why are you selling it?" As a seller, you want to be well prepared and rehearsed for this question—never make it up on the fly. An excellent technique to use for all the questions illustrated here is to embed your answers into your consciousness. You do this by following this simple formula: 1) write out the question and your answer; 2) read your answer out loud until you have committed it to memory.

The second question is, "How much are you asking for the business?" Never volunteer your number up front. Simply provide the facts describing your business's financial performance and some key strengths regarding your recurring customers, systems, and processes, and then ask the potential buyer what they feel a business with those traits should sell for. Put the onus on the buyer to offer the first number. You will immediately know if they are serious and have done their homework on business value in the current marketplace.

The next question you can expect a buyer to ask is, "What makes your company different than your competitors?" The buyer is trying to understand what makes you unique and how they can effectively differentiate the business in the marketplace if they buy it. If there is no differentiation, there is no unique value.

Another common question is, "How would you grow the business if you were in my shoes?" The buyer is trying to understand what you think the business needs. This is a bit of a trick question. Remember that if a buyer can find enough flaws in a business they want to buy, the buyer will attempt to use those flaws to negotiate the price down. Don't fall victim to this.

Finally, you need to be prepared to answer the question, "Will your customers and employees stay if I buy the business?" The answer should always be truthful and positive. The bottom line is that customers and employees will be wary when they learn of an ownership change, wondering how the change will affect them. If nothing affects them negatively, there is a strong likelihood that none of the customers or employees will leave because they have no reason or justification for change. If, however, the new buyer endeavors to change everything, it's likely that customers and employees will also affect a change and leave unless the perceived benefit is much greater for them than leaving—but many will leave anyway because they are afraid of change.

Remember, if the buyer perceives that you need to sell for a particular reason, they're going to be very hard negotiators, right? They're going to try and get you down because they will perceive that your need to sell is higher than their need to buy, right? They smell opportunity. How you answer these questions can make the difference between getting a deal done and not getting a deal done.

GETTING THE DEAL DONE

*"Don't bunt. Aim out of the ballpark.
Aim for the company of immortals."*
—David Ogilvy

At this stage of the game, you will have provided your business broker with all the information relating to your company, including your balance sheets, profit and loss statements, inventory analysis, at least three years of tax returns, and an outline of your payables and receivables. Be prepared to provide updated copies of these reports every 30 days throughout the sales process. Even once an offer has been tendered and accepted, the buyer's bank or financing source will want to be assured that the company is still as financially sound as it was when initially represented.

The buyer will also require proof that your sales taxes, social security, and unemployment taxes have been paid and are up to date, your quarterly income taxes are paid and up to date, and that there are no outstanding liens or tax obligations relating to the company.

If the buyer is seeking a loan through the Small Business Association (SBA loan), you will be required to provide IRS transcripts of your previous three years' tax returns. I would suggest obtaining these returns early in the process just in case there are any unforeseen glitches. I learned this the hard way.

My company was scheduled to close on January 2, 2019. The buyer's lender requested that I provide the IRS transcripts in early December. I completed the form the day it was requested and forwarded it to the IRS. It was mailed back to me three weeks later, stating that it could not be accepted because it was not legible. Mind you, this was a pre-printed form with all information filled out via computer. The only handwriting on the document was my signature! This was December 21, 2018, the day the government shut down. I sent it back immediately and then couldn't reach anyone at the IRS for several weeks.

After dozens of phone calls and hours of time invested, I was told that the IRS didn't even recognize my EIN and had no record of my tax returns. My returns were always completed by a professional CPA firm, and they had records of the e-filings and IRS receipt and acceptance. The IRS had also cashed the checks for my tax payments. I won't go into the entire story at this time, but the bottom line was a glitch with my S-Corporation filing in 2015 that was never brought to our attention. The IRS had assigned us a new EIN without ever notifying us.

Needless to say, this was a nightmare to untangle. I met with tax advocates and contacted a variety of offices in

Washington, D.C. I was instructed to fax information, only to learn that the day they asked me to fax something the IRS was converting from fax to e-mail and nothing could go through—no fax, no e-mail. We were in limbo. The bottom line is we could not close the company on January 2 or even February 2. We finally received the audited return transcripts and were able to close on March 7. Can you imagine the stress on me, the buyer, and the employees? It was something no one could have ever anticipated.

When I initially contracted with the business broker, he stated that we had the most detailed package of solid business information (including financials and tax records) that he had ever seen. It just goes to show, you never know what snags you might run into, so begin compiling documentation early in the process.

Once the marketing materials have been provided to potential buyers, the broker will reach out to answer any questions and to query as to the candidate's interest in purchasing the company. Once a candidate expresses interest, the broker then provides a very detailed questionnaire to be completed by the buyer. Once the potential buyer has submitted this information, the broker will research the information provided, assess that information provided is true and accurate, and set up an appointment to meet and interview the potential buyer.

After this interview, if the broker determines that the potential buyer is a viable candidate for purchasing the company and the candidate has expressed interest in moving forward with the purchase process, the broker will move to the next step of the selling process.

When the potential buyer has decided to move forward with the purchase of the company, it is customary to submit a personal and confidential letter of intent to the seller. The letter of intent summarizes the general terms and conditions of a contemplated acquisition of the company and usually includes the following:

- Purchase price
- Transaction, which includes projected closing date
- Inspection, with seller to provide various due diligence requests
- Settlement
- Closing credit
- Transition with an agreed-upon transition plan between seller and buyer
- Employment arrangements that outlines employees who would be offered employment upon the sale of the company
- Conditions set forth by the buyer
- Exclusivity period, the amount of time in which the seller agrees to stop marketing activities while the buyer is completing due diligence
- Binding confidentiality. Buyer agrees not to discuss or disclose the contemplated transaction with anyone other than those on their transaction team. Seller also agrees not to discuss or disclose the contemplated transaction with anyone other than those on their transaction team.
- Binding provisions. States that the letter of intent is intended to be a statement of the general terms and conditions of the contemplated transaction. It

shall not be construed in any way as an obligation or binding agreement for the parties to consummate the transaction.

The letter of intent is the prelude to a formal purchase agreement. The purchase agreement (offer) is a much more detailed document outlining terms and conditions relating to the purchase of the company.

The initial offer is carefully reviewed by the broker. After the broker has reviewed the offer, a meeting is scheduled between the broker and the seller to discuss the offer. After this meeting, the offer is submitted to the seller's attorney. You should utilize an attorney who specializes solely in the sale of businesses. Furthermore, you want to be judicious in submitting items to the attorney as any time spent in the process adds up to more billable hours.

The seller will also be required to provide true and complete copies of their financial documents as set forth in monthly reports for the three years up to and including the date of sale. Most importantly, all of the tax returns and reports of the seller are required by law to be filed on or before the date of the agreement and have been duly and timely filed, and all taxes shown as due thereon have been paid. Once an offer is tendered and accepted, you will enter the final stage leading to the closing.

DUE DILIGENCE

Once the seller and buyer have agreed to the terms of the sale, the process enters the due diligence period. The price, terms, and timing are set, and both parties will develop a purchase agreement, which ultimately transfers ownership of the business.

This is also the time when your roles reverse. Up to this point, you've generated information and documents for the buyer. Now, the buyer comes to you requesting specific information they need to finalize the transaction. It's your responsibility to provide the information desired.

When the buyer presents the list of required documents for the due diligence period, the process of locating, copying, conveying, and then addressing any issues within the documents can overwhelm the seller. This is where your team really adds value.

A professionally managed team prepares for this request from the beginning. Your broker will ask you to gather this information while your business is being marketed. This gives you time to locate, review, and take care of any issues with the documents. Then, when it's time to share them with the buyer, they're already organized and reflect the present state of the business.

A key part of the due diligence period involves preparing, negotiating, and completing the formal purchase agreement. As a seller, it is to your advantage to have the buyer and their team prepare the purchase agreement. This puts the majority of the time and expense involved with the document preparation on the buyer's team. The seller's team's responsibility is to review and comment on the document. Thus, the seller is never in a position to give more than is required and never has to accept anything other than what they desire.

The purchase agreement is a lengthy document. (Ours was eighteen pages.) Articles typically addressed in the purchase agreement include but are not limited to:

- Purchase and sale, purchase price, closing
- Inspection period
- Representations and warranties of seller and principal
- Representations and warranties of buyer
- Obligations of the parties
- Conditions to buyer's obligations
- Conditions to seller's obligations
- Closing, closing date
- Post-closing covenants
- Indemnification
- Termination
- Other agreements

There may also be several schedules attached to the agreement relating to various aspects of the sale.

Your attorney will immediately be able to spot holes in the offer that may adversely affect you, the seller. It is a complex dance between the buyer and the seller as both parties are seeking an agreement that is most beneficial to their initiative. There is give-and-take involved in the process, and negotiations can go back and forth numerous times. Keep in mind that each time an attorney reviews the document, the clock is ticking, and expenses are mounting. Try to look at the offer objectively from all sides before asking your attorney to provide revisions. Some of the key items that may be addressed in various schedule attachments could include:

- Determining rights under all contracts that are used in the business on which the seller is a party.
- Determining the allocation of various security deposits, lease deposits, utility deposits, and other prepaid assets arising out of the conduct of the business.
- Supplies and inventory relating to the business that will be transferred with the sale.
- Intellectual and intangible assets, including trade secrets, telephone numbers, websites, social media, domain names, IP addresses, trade names, logos, all stored data, owned computer software, and similar items used in connection with the business.
- Assets that will be excluded from the sale.
- The buyer-assumed and excluded liabilities relating to existing contracted businesses.
- Schedule of all work in progress, accounts receivable, and customer deposits that will be prorated with the express agreement of both buyer and seller. These include open staged contracts and open un-staged contracts, which is business that has been scheduled but not yet completed at the time of closing.
- Allocation of purchase price. This is one of the **most important** elements of the offer to purchase. A portion of the purchase price is allocated toward furniture, fixtures, equipment, and other tangible personal property. The balance is allocated to personal goodwill (the intangible aspects of the business). As a seller, you want the highest amount of the purchase price allocated toward personal goodwill because, at this writing, it is currently at a much lower tax rate than the tangible personal property. This is an

area that involves give and take. It's a fine balance between buyer and seller, as a tax situation that benefits the seller typically gives the buyer a higher tax obligation. This is why it is critical to have a good accountant involved in the sale of your company.
- Complete list of each lease pursuant to which seller leases, as lessor or lessee, and any real property interest.
- Any litigation set forth relating to actions, claims, proceedings, grievances, and investigations against the seller within the previous five years as of the closing date.
- Complete list of each contract and commitment of seller that is material to the operations, assets, business, or financial condition of the seller or the business.
- List containing information relating to all employees of seller, their respective titles, rates of pay (including, separately, base pay and any incentive or commission plans), and accrued vacation or sick time.

As mentioned, these are just some of the schedules that may be included as a part of the purchase agreement. Depending on your attorney, location or country of your business operations, tax status, and other miscellaneous factors, these or other schedules may or may not be included in the purchase agreement.

The seller will also be required to provide true and complete copies of their financial documents as set forth in monthly reports for the three years up to and including the date of sale. Most importantly, all of the tax returns and reports of the seller are required by law to be filed on or before the date of the agreement and have been duly and timely filed, and all taxes shown as due thereon have been paid.

At this point, you, with the assistance of your attorney, will begin compiling the information requested in the various schedules. Depending on how much initial or advance planning you have undertaken, this can be an extremely laborious process. This is also an area where your attorney will spend many hours reviewing and fine-tuning the information. Once these are completed, they will be attached to the purchase agreement and submitted for the final offer.

Once all parties have reviewed the purchase agreement and modifications have been made and agreed upon, the final offer is submitted to the seller and is signed (executed) by both the seller and buyer. This is now a binding agreement to purchase your company.

Keep in mind that there will most likely be an article of termination included as a condition of the agreement. In most cases, termination outlined in the agreement can be effected by mutual consent of the buyer and seller, by either the buyer or seller if the closing has not occurred by the contracted closing date, or by either the buyer or seller if there has been a material breach by either party in any material representation, warranty, or covenant set forth in the agreement that is not cured within ten business days after such other party has been notified of the intent to terminate the agreement pursuant to this clause.

The end is in sight! So much information has been shared, the negotiation is over, and now all that is left is signing the papers and transferring the money. Well, that is the way it's supposed to work. However, it's not always the case.

Closing is often a fire drill where all parties frantically take one last look through every document and representation and make sure all the i's are dotted and all the t's are crossed. The market is littered with stories of everything falling apart at the last second. And many of these stories are true—most often with DIY sellers. Why? Generally, because expectations and emotions are high, and both sides realize that the buyer holds all the cards. So, if the buyer doesn't get what they want, they walk. Sellers dislike being held hostage.

It doesn't have to be that way. Sellers with a team have experience on their side, and experience teaches them to read the signs for approaching hazards. The experience again demonstrates its value in the closing stage. The team can spot warning signs and know how to keep everyone focused on the desired outcome—a smooth business transfer. It's trite but true: As long as everyone stays focused on the goal, the goal gets achieved.

Closing dates involve both parties signing the final papers and verifying funds wired (the most common method of money transfer). In a properly managed transaction, the agreements will have been reviewed and agreed upon (and more often, even signed) before the closing date. All the necessary licenses, permits, or transfers have taken place (or are scheduled to take place on the appropriate date), and all verifications are in place. Funds have been verified on deposit and scheduled for wire transfer. Notices are prepared, and if employees aren't aware, an all-hands meeting is scheduled. Customer communications and press releases are reviewed, approved, and ready for disbursement. All systems are GO.

Then it's time to inform the employees, suppliers, and customers. It works best if both you and the buyer make these announcements together and in person. The buyer should be prepared to address what, if any, changes will take place for employees, including job responsibilities, reporting, compensation, benefits, and so on. Suppliers may require renewed credit detail and supply specifics. Customers (particularly those who are strategic or represent a significant share of sales) will often want to know that things like price, delivery, and performance will remain satisfactory, and they often want to understand the new owner's vision of the future. Preparing for this announcement will go a long way to ensure a smooth transition.

If you are lucky enough to make it through the entire process without employees getting wind of the potential sale, kudos to you. Immediately after closing, you will need to sit down with your employees, assure them of a smooth transition, thank them for their service, and introduce them to the new owner. You may want to provide them with final bonuses or gifts to show your appreciation for their hard work.

One of the elements you provided to your broker was a list of current clients and the revenue each of these clients brings into your firm each year. The person looking to purchase your company will be relying on these folks remaining clients of the firm and on said revenue. We had a client who generated over $250,000 per year of revenue for our firm. Can you imagine if this relationship was lost before the close of the sale? The person purchasing your company is relying on those clients remaining loyal to the brand. This is why confidentiality is so important. If, by chance, you do lose a key client prior to closing, you are obligated to inform the buyer of the situation.

Once we knew the sale was clear to close, I personally contacted key clients to thank them for their business and express how much they meant to us. At this point, I also provided information on the new owner and set up a time for them to meet the new owner. I call this the passing of the torch. This allows the new owner to get a feel for your relationship with the client and makes it much more comfortable for everyone involved in the process. If you have an extremely large client base, you may want to send out a letter of appreciation and provide them with the new contact information.

THE CLOSING

The closing will be determined based on the source of funding the buyer is utilizing. In our case, the buyer was putting up a percentage of cash, and the balance would be paid out through a government-guaranteed loan through the Small Business Association. Banks are required to request and review a plethora of the seller's financial and tax information prior to approving the buyer for the loan.

As previously mentioned in an earlier chapter, this includes three years of audited federal tax transcripts. This type of transcript cannot be downloaded from the IRS website, so you will need to budget for some time to allow for receipt. If the buyer is utilizing a lender, the closing is typically held at the lender's offices. Attendees of the closing generally include the seller, seller's attorney, business broker, buyer, buyer's attorney, notary public, and the lender.

There are numerous documents to be reviewed, signed, and notarized relating to the sale of the business. These may include the following:

- Amendment to purchase agreement. This document generally outlines the financing and disbursement of funds, including post-closing disbursement agreement, promissory note, security agreement, and personal guarantee.
- Escrow agreement. Generally, a good faith sum is held in escrow by the seller's attorney. This agreement, signed by the buyer, releases said funds to the seller ("principal").
- Closing statement. This outlines the purchase price, funds coming from the buyer, from the lender, previously escrowed funds, prorations schedule, closing credits, and any additional items that will be paid out of closing proceeds.
- Security agreement. This document outlines the obligations of the borrower to the secured party and basically protects the lender.
- Personal guarantee. This must be signed by the purchaser(s) and notarized.
- Promissory note. Buyer ("maker") promises to pay seller ("payee") the agreed-upon funds. This also outlines any interest, prepayment, security, default, etc.

- Assignment and assumption agreement. Seller ("assignor") assigns, transfers, and conveys unto buyer ("assignee") all right, title, and interest that assignor has or may have in and to the purchased contracts and assignor hereby assigns, transfers, and delegates to assignee the assumed liabilities.
- Bill of sale. By this bill of sale and in accordance with the purchase agreement, the principal hereby sells, assigns, transfers, conveys, and delivers to the buyer and the buyer's successors all the principal's right, title, and interest in and to all the personal goodwill, as that term is defined in the purchase agreement.
- Assignment and bill of sale. Through this agreement, seller ("assignor") does hereby sell, convey, transfer, assign, and deliver to buyer ("assignee") all right, title, and interest in and to the transferred assets free and clear of all liens.

As mentioned previously, prior to marketing the company, the seller and business broker will determine assets and goodwill items that will be transferred with the sale of the company. The seller may choose not to convey certain items as part of the sale. An example of this may be the company trademark.

In our case, we were moving out of state with plans of possibly starting another staging business. After thirteen years in business, our brand was well known throughout the country due to the receipt of numerous national awards. As part of the sale, we offered the buyer the right to utilize the company trademark through a formal license agreement. This license agreement was another document that was executed at the closing table.

As you can see, there are a multitude of documents to be signed and executed at the closing table. These documents should be completed at least twenty-four hours prior to closing and provided to both attorneys, buyer, seller, and business broker for review. Even when reviewed in advance, plan to spend a couple of hours at the closing table.

PASSING THE BATON

The baton has been passed to the new owner. You will feel a profound sense of relief and accomplishment. It's time to celebrate! It's also a good idea to have planned in advance exactly what you will do tomorrow. You have probably been so used to going to bed thinking about the business and waking up ready to jump right back into it. You will probably feel a bit disoriented at first. That's why it's important to have a plan in place. Plan to take that well-deserved tropical vacation, visit the grandkids, schedule a massage, schedule lunch with friends, read those books you have been saving for just this moment. Fill your calendar to the brim. The last thing you want to do is wake up the day after the sale has been finalized and say to yourself, "What am I going to do today? What am I going to do with the rest of my life?" Just don't forget the time you have committed to being available to help the new owner through the transition. This is one of the most important aspects of her achieving continued success in the business.

SUPPORTING THE NEW BUSINESS OWNER

A section of the purchase agreement will have addressed how much time (if any) the seller will be available to assist the buyer (new owner) in the running of the business. This is generally determined by the level of knowledge and competence the buyer has relating to the staging business and industry. If the buyer has previously owned a staging business or was a key employee of this or another company, she may not require significant training or sharing of knowledge from the seller. On the other hand, if the buyer is new to the staging industry, she may need significant assistance from the seller. All of this will have been addressed and negotiated prior to closing.

In my case, I made myself available either via phone, e-mail, or in-person (as needed) for a period of thirty consecutive days. Each sales scenario will require a different level of commitment from the previous owner. That said, you should plan to assist with the smooth transition of ownership.

WRAPPING UP THE LOOSE ENDS

Once you have closed on the company, there are still a few more details that need to be addressed before you close this chapter of your life.

THE IRS

If you have closed on the business prior to the third quarter, you may be required to file a short-year tax return. Your accountant should have already calculated your expected tax obligation prior to closing. You will file and submit your projected taxes at this time. Depending on your business structure, your accountant will complete and file a Schedule K. If your business is on a calendar year filing, your accountant will prepare and file the final year-end tax return for both federal and state taxes. At this time, your financials for the balance of the year will be factored into the equation, and you may either owe additional taxes or be eligible to receive a tax refund based on over-projections.

Be sure that you retain your company's tax records and receipts for a period of seven years, as you could be audited at any time. Do not leave your records with the new owner of the company.

ATTORNEY

Your attorney will assist in filing the required tax clearance letter with the Department of Revenue, and depending on your state or country, you may be required (as we were) to file articles of termination of an LLC, dissolution documents including state-mandated notice of winding up for a limited liability company, a notice of winding up to all creditors of and claimants against your LLC, which is posted in public records, and a request for tax clearance from your state. Once your business has transferred to the new owner and the aforesaid documents have been submitted, your attorney will provide you with a letter to memorialize the completion of legal services relating to the sale of the business.

THE NEW OWNER

As outlined above, you want to do everything in your power to set the new owner up for continued success.

They purchased the company with the expectation of maintaining current revenue levels and even taking the business to the next level. In these days of social media, you will be able to see just about everything that is taking place posted on Facebook, Instagram, and other platforms. It is human nature to compare what the new owner is doing to what you have done or would have done with a particular home staging or situation.

Take a deep breath and remember that there isn't one path to success. That said, if you notice something that could be a detriment to the new owner's success, you owe it to them to share. But, before sharing your thoughts, be certain that it is truly something that could negatively impact their new company. They may just be doing things differently, and sometimes, different is better.

This was very difficult for me. After thirteen years in the business, I couldn't help but critique the photos that were shared online. I often said to myself things like, "Why did she do that?" and, "I wouldn't have put that coffee table with that end table." I didn't share this with the new owner, but it did bother me. I had to take a good hard look within and tell myself to let go. It wasn't my company anymore, and it wasn't any of my business. I had to take a break from following the page, and you may, too.

You want to see the new owner maintain, grow, and take the business that you built to new levels and continue the legacy. The new owner may not sustain relationships with some of your previous customers. That's okay. Not every personality works well with everyone else. She will build new relationships that work well for her and her team. The best advice I can give is to not take it personally.

It is her company now. You have built your dream, sold it for a profit, and are reaping the rewards of your success. Now, it's her turn.

FINALE! ENJOYING THE REWARDS

"It always seems impossible until it's done."
—Nelson Mandela

Whew! The business is finally sold and closed. As you can see, it is quite the process. Now it is time to take the check to the bank and enjoy the fruits of your labors.

At this point, if you had been in the staging business several years prior to selling, you may want to think about offering staging training for other stagers or continuing education courses for real estate agents. You may want to start some other type of business or do like I did: retire to sunny Sarasota! Whatever you decide, the world is your oyster. You can be proud that you built a fabulous business and were able to sell it. Did you know that 20 percent of new businesses don't make it through the first year? By the end of the fifth year, 50 percent have failed. After ten years, only about one-third of businesses have survived. You are one of the few, the proud, the brave. Celebrate your success!

ACKNOWLEDGMENTS

My heartfelt thanks to my daughter and right-hand business partner, Courtney Schomburg. We had a fabulous, wild ride, and while we were always extremely close, this experience brought us a closer bond than either of us ever could have imagined. There were times early on when we had about $3 in the checkbook, and we continued to believe and soldier on.

Courtney made it her goal/mission to sign up for just about every professional staging course offered around the country. She's the one who prepared the award documentation and submitted photos to the various staging organizations, which resulted in us receiving numerous top staging industry awards. She's the one who had the vision to sell the company and for us all to move to Florida and start a new chapter. Even after the sale of the company, she has selflessly given her time as national chairperson of the Real Estate Staging Association.

I would be remiss if I didn't acknowledge my wonderful son-in-law, Jon Schomburg. After we were in business a few years, Courtney and I realized that we couldn't continue to do it alone. Both Courtney and I are creative types with virtually no desire to handle accounting, billing, or anything to do with math. We convinced Jon to leave his career in banking and take over the operations, freeing us to do what we did best: stage houses. Jon was instrumental in developing the processes, spreadsheets, and procedures that enabled our company to stand out and be sold for top dollar.

A special thank you to the Home Builder's Association of Greater Saint Louis. If it weren't for the numerous contacts I had made through the association in the years prior to starting the business, we would have never enjoyed the type of success we had from day number one. A big thanks also goes out to the Saint Louis Association of Realtors and Saint Charles Association of Realtors for allowing me to teach dozens of continuing education courses for realtors to educate them on the benefits of home staging. Also, thank you to the hundreds of realtors, investors, and homebuilders who supported us during our thirteen-year run. We owe our success to all of you and thank you from the bottom of our hearts.

Thank you to Christine Rae, who provided my entire team with professional Certified Staging Professional training and for allowing me to, in turn, provide training to others through the CSP platform. Also, thank you to the Real Estate Staging Association (RESA) for continuing to support, promote, grow, and develop the home staging industry through their code of ethics, annual conventions, and educational platforms.

We are eternally grateful to Steve Denny, who held our hand and guided us through the entire process. Steve was instrumental not only in setting us on the right path to our new life journey but also in creating this book.

Finally, a huge heartfelt thank you to my rock, Johnsie Connolly, who believed in me even when I didn't believe in myself. He didn't blink when I suggested I give up my solid career and six-figure income and benefits to pursue the dream of starting a home staging company. He handed me $5,000 and said, "I know you can do this," and we did!

The staging industry has grown and changed so much since 2007 and will continue to do so as time goes on. I can't wait to see the companies that are industry leaders right now take their companies into the future and, when the time is right for them, sell their companies seamlessly and for top dollar.

ABOUT THE AUTHORS

Award-winning staging professional **Liz Connolly** has been a prominent figure in the staging industry since early 2007. At that time, Liz founded INhance IT! Home Staging in Saint Louis, and through that company, staged over 5,000 properties. In early 2019, Liz sold the Saint Louis division and relocated with her family to Sarasota, Florida, where she has recently founded "From Staged to Sold," a firm assisting individuals interested in selling their home staging businesses.

INhance IT! received dozens of national and international industry awards and accolades. In 2017, 2018, and 2019, INhance IT! was recognized by RESA as one of the top ten staging teams in North America, and Liz was recognized as Top Ten Professional Stager in both 2016 and 2017.

Liz is a RESA-Pro member, a member of the Institute of Residential Marketing, and a Master Certified Staging Professional. Liz holds the following designations:

- International Master Certified Staging Professional
- CSP Luxury Staging Specialist
- CSP Occupied Staging Specialist
- CSP Vacant Staging Specialist
- CSP Residential Renovation Project Manager
- CSP Approved Mentor
- CSP Vacant Staging & Builder Project Instructor
- Staging and Design Professional (Staging Studio)

Liz has been a RESA-approved CE instructor since 2019 and has been a guest speaker at RESA-con. She has appeared on numerous panels, television promotions, and has authored articles for a wide array of industry publications.

How to connect with Liz
e-mail: Liz@sellingstaging.com
Facebook
Linkedin.com/Liz-Connolly

Steven Denny is a partner with Innovative Business Advisors, a mergers and acquisition firm specializing in serving companies of $1 million to $50 million in enterprise value. The firm provides M/A services, business valuation services, exit planning, and specialized coaching services designed to help business owners grow enterprise value and profits.

Steve began his career in business development with a Fortune 100 firm and was one of the youngest vice presidents in his industry. He eventually attained a senior executive role with national responsibilities. After twenty-five years of service in the industry, he retired and founded ABN, a business consulting and brokerage business in Saint Louis, Missouri, in 2005. In 2018, Steve merged his firm with Innovative Business Advisors and was recognized as one of the "Best M&A Providers in Saint Louis."

Steve and his wife Debi reside in suburban Saint Louis and enjoy spending time with their children and grandchildren.

About the Authors

How to connect with Steve:
Web: www.*innovativeba.com*
Email: *sdenny@innovativeba.com*
Phone: *(800) 767-2465*
Linkedin.com/steven-denny-iba

ABOUT YOU DON'T KNOW WHAT YOU DON'T KNOW™

The phrase "You don't know what you don't know" is used often in our practice at IBA LLC to describe an experience and process that many of our clients go through for the first time when we work with them. It describes a gap in knowledge that comes from a lack of experience. We work with clients to make the experience as fruitful as possible.

My partner, Terry Lammers, and I decided to trademark this phrase and use it to write a series of books designed to share knowledge with business owners. Our vision is to write about things we know are not well known—buying and selling businesses, valuing businesses, working with trusted advisers, etc. We hope our books will help fill that gap in knowledge.

This book is the third in a series that we expect will be much larger in number. Our publisher, Nancy Erickson of Stonebrook Publishing, has developed an incredibly useful process for us to write these books, and if you have a book in you, we strongly encourage you to go to *www. TheBookProfessor.com* and learn more about how to get your idea on paper and into the marketplace.

We also invite you to go to *www.YouDontKnowWhat YouDontKnow.com* and register. As a registrant, you will be invited to review future books and be able to download and benefit from additional resources that we design to be complementary to the book series. You can also connect with us there, share your feedback, and ask us any questions that you may have.

Thanks so much for being a reader. We are honored to serve you.

We encourage you to share the book and resources with others.

www.ingramcontent.com/pod-product-compliance
Lightning Source LLC
Chambersburg PA
CBHW050506240426
43673CB00031B/490/J